NORTHERN ITALIAN

Cooking

by Biba Caggiano

Contents

ANOTHER BEST-SELLING VOLUME FROM HPBooks®
Publisher: Rick Bailey; Editorial Director: Elaine R. Woodard; Editor: Veronica Durie; Art Director: Don Burton; Book Design and Illustrations: Ken Heiden; Typography: Cindy Coatsworth, Joanne Nociti, Michelle Carter; Book Manufacture: Anthony B. Narducci; Food Stylist: Mable Hoffman; Photography: George de Gennaro Studios

Published by HPBooks, Inc., P.O. Box 5367, Tucson, AZ 85703   602/888-2150
ISBN 0-89586-119-4; ISBN 0-89586-127-5 (cloth)
Library of Congress Catalog Card No. 81-82276
©1981 HPBooks, Inc.   Printed in U.S.A.
3rd Printing

Acknowledgements

"No man is an island entire of itself." (John Donne)

This book would not have happened without the contributions of many people. My mother taught me the best of family cooking. My friends in Bologna: Dante Casari of Ristorante Dante; Gianni Sarti of Ristorante Bacco; Enzo Venturi of Ristorante Rodrigo; and Athos Degliesposti and Pippo Bondi of Ristorante Diana. I want to thank all my students. I greatly appreciate the help of two special friends: Darrell Corti, wine and food expert, and Dave Berkley, wine consultant to the White House, who suggested wines for this book. I am grateful to George de Gennaro and his staff, who through their photography transformed my food into works of art. Finally, I must thank my husband Vincent and my daughters Carla and Paola, for all their support, patience and love.

Cover photo: Green & Yellow Tortelloni with Ricotta Cheese & Parsley, page 52.

Fabulous Food of Northern Italy

*I*f anyone had suggested to me five years ago that I should write a cookbook, I would have laughed and thought it a preposterous idea. How little do we know! It all began when I was persuaded by several friends to teach them some of my dishes. The classes were a great success. Then I was asked to teach at a local cooking school. These classes were also well received. Soon demands for my classes came from other cities. Again the classes were very popular.

The reason? The food of northern Italy with its enormous range, simplicity and great classic dishes, had won the hearts of my students.

My classes were conducted in a simple and informal manner without fancy tricks or hard techniques to master. The object was to share my knowledge and to dispel myths about Italian cuisine. My students were not intimidated. They went home and cooked. They made pasta, polenta, gnocchi and risotto. They cooked all the dishes we covered in the classes, whether simple or elaborate. They learned at the classes and in their own kitchens that northern Italian food is simply outstanding and outstandingly simple!

This book draws its recipes from every region north of Tuscany, with the emphasis on the food of my region, Emilia-Romagna. Bologna, the capital, is instantly associated with food and is considered by many the gastronomical capital of Italy. A few dishes have been included that originated in other regions. You will find them here because they have become national rather than regional and are served throughout the country.

Anyone who has traveled in Italy will tell you that Italian cuisine is unbelievably varied. Before the unification of Italy in 1861, each city-state had different rulers, cultures, customs and dialects. Each also had its own distinctive cuisine. Italian food is basically very simple with its roots drawn from peasant cooking. For centuries Italy has had Popes, Courts and great families who have brought a more sophisticated and lavish style to the cuisine. The blending of these two styles of cooking has resulted in *la buona cucina casalinga,* good home cooking.

The cooking styles of northern Italy are as diversified as the Italian landscape. The cooking of Piedmont, for example, is very different from the cooking of Emilia-Romagna. Piedmont is dominated by mountains. Its cuisine is robust, sober and elegant. Game, truffles and meats braised in full-bodied wines are all part of Piedmont cooking. This region is also the greatest producer of rice in Europe.

By contrast, Emilia-Romagna is located in one of the flattest parts of Italy with the Apennines in the northwest and the Adriatic Sea to the east. This area is known for its generous use of butter and for pork products that find their way into innumerable dishes. Emilia-Romagna leads Italy in the production of wheat and consequently is famous for the quality of its pasta.

Cooking is second nature for most Italians. Even though certain guidelines are important, there is no place in Italian cooking for rigid rules or formulas. The love of cooking and eating is reflected in everyday life. Shopping is generally done daily to assure the freshest possible ingredients. Great care is taken in the selection of these ingredients. The Italian cook spends as much time and effort on preparing a family meal as she would if cooking for guests. By 11 a.m. she is preparing a sauce or *ragù* to be served over pasta at 1 p.m.

The country shuts down at 12:30 p.m. every day. Italians jump into their cars and fight the chaotic city traffic to reach their homes in order to enjoy lunch, the most important meal of the day. The family gathers around the table and the meal becomes a celebration of the food itself and the traditions behind it.

Serving a meal properly is almost as important as cooking it well. In an Italian meal, portions are generally small. Pasta, soup or risotto is served as a first course. Meat or fish follows accompanied by one or two vegetables. Then a simple salad is served with an olive oil and vinegar or lemon dressing. Fresh fruit and espresso coffee end the meal. Dessert is only served on special occasions.

Despite the occasional substitution of one ingredient for another, all the dishes in this book can be reproduced successfully outside Italy. Italian cuisine is a skillful blending of ingredients that complement one another. Once you have done that, you have mastered the art of Italian cooking. After all, good food is not the property of Italian people alone. Good food is like good wine. It needs love, dedication and a touch of artistry to be outstanding.

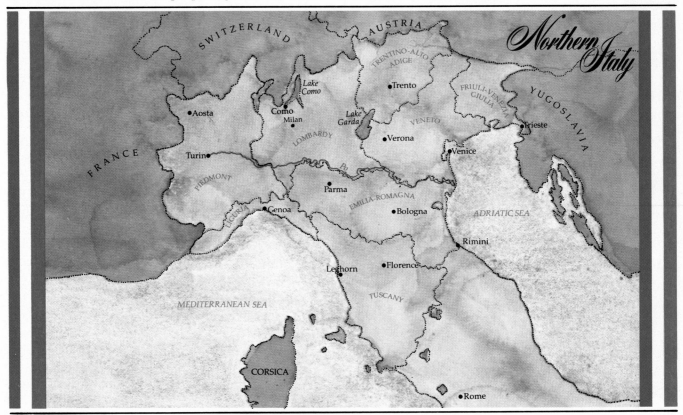

Some Basic Ingredients

Because Italian cuisine is basically simple, each ingredient plays a very important role. Certain dishes cannot be made without a specific ingredient and still be considered authentic. While many ingredients are vital, I also realize that some are often unavailable in rural areas. I urge you to go the extra mile to find an important ingredient and to substitute only if you must.

Basil—Fresh basil is probably the most popular Italian herb. The only substitute is home-preserved basil. Basil leaves can be preserved between layers of coarse salt in tightly sealed jars. They lose some of their green color, but retain the flavor. Basil can also be preserved in olive oil.

Broth—Broth is an important ingredient in Italian cooking. Risotto, for example, cannot be made without it. Broth is also used in sauces, stews and braised meats. Make large batches and freeze it.

Butter—Butter is widely used in northern Italy. It is preferred for cooking instead of olive oil.

Fontina Cheese—Fontina is a delicious cheese from Piedmont. Its delicate flavor enhances many Italian dishes. Substitute with stronger-flavored Danish fontina only if absolutely necessary.

Garlic—Garlic is widely used in Italian cooking but it should not be abused. Many dishes that call for garlic, need only a hint of it. Choose a large head of garlic with firm, unwrinkled cloves.

Gorgonzola Cheese—This blue-vein cheese comes from Lombardy. Gorgonzola is pungent with a creamy consistency. Substitute blue cheese, preferably Oregon Blue, only if absolutely necessary.

Marsala Wine—The best Marsala wine comes from Marsala in Sicily. Dry and sweet types are available. Use dry Marsala for cooking. Its aromatic flavor is essential to many dishes. American Marsala wine is sweeter than the Italian and should be used with discretion. Substitute dry sherry if Marsala is unavailable.

Mozzarella Cheese—One of Italy's favorite cheeses, the best mozzarella is made from the curd of water-buffalo milk. It is generally stored in water and does not keep very long. It has a creamy and delicate taste. Substitute domestic mozzarella.

Oil for frying—For deep-frying use any light-flavored vegetable oil.

Olive Oil—In choosing an olive oil, look for a nice green color and a pleasing taste and fragrance. Some of the best Italian olive oils come from Tuscany, Umbria and Liguria. Extra virgin olive oil which is the product of the first pressing of the olives is considered the best. Store olive oil in a tightly capped bottle in a cool, dark place. Use olive oil within a few months or it may turn rancid.

Pancetta—Pancetta is the same cut of pork as bacon. It is cured with salt and is not smoked. It comes rolled up like a large salami. Widely used in Italian cooking, especially in Emilia-Romagna, it is vital to many dishes. If available, buy a large quantity, cut into several pieces and freeze it. You can substitute domestic bacon for pancetta. It must be blanched in boiling water for two to three minutes to reduce the smoky flavor. Fresh side pork can also be used.

Parmesan Cheese—Italian cuisine would not be the same without this cheese. Parmesan is produced in an area between Parma and Reggio-Emilia. It is made under strict regulations. When buying Parmesan, look for *Parmigiano Reggiano* stamped on the crust. The cheese should be straw-yellow and crumbly and moist inside. It is expensive, but a little goes a long way. Buy a small piece and grate only what you need. Wrap the remaining cheese tightly in foil and store in the refrigerator. Domestic Parmesan is subject to different standards and not aged as long. If necessary, domestic Parmesan can be used. Do not use the grated Parmesan sold at the supermarket unless you have no other choice.

Parsley—If available, use the large, flat-leaf Italian parsley. Parsley is widely used in Italian cooking. It is a good source of vitamins A and C and also iron.

Prosciutto—Prosciutto is uncooked, unsmoked ham. It is salted, air-cured and aged a minimum of one year. Italian prosciutto is usually much sweeter than the American counterpart. Prosciutto is widely used in Italian cooking and as an *anti-pasto*. Domestic prosciutto is an acceptable substitute.

Rice—Italian rice is short and thick-grained. It is perfect for risotto. Imported Italian rice such as *arborio* is available in Italian groceries and specialty stores. California short-grain pearl rice can be substituted for arborio.

Ricotta Cheese—Domestic ricotta is acceptable. It has a creamier consistency than Italian ricotta and is more watery. Never substitute cottage cheese for ricotta.

Rosemary—Rosemary is deliciously aromatic. It is excellent with roasts or in marinades. Dried rosemary is perfectly acceptable.

Sage—Sage is at its best when used with poultry and game. Use dried sage sparingly because its strong flavor can be overwhelming.

Tomatoes—There is no doubt that a sauce made from meaty sun-ripened tomatoes is unbeatable. Good-quality canned tomatoes make a good substitute. If possible, choose an imported Italian variety. If using domestic canned plum tomatoes, try several brands to find one that suits your taste.

Vinegar—Use a good, unflavored wine vinegar.

Wild Italian Mushrooms—These are one of the glorious elements in Italian gastronomy. They grow under chestnut trees and are abundant in the fall and spring. Drying wild mushrooms preserves their distinctive flavor. Dried wild Italian mushrooms are available in Italian groceries and gourmet stores.

Wine—If a wine is good enough to drink, it is good enough for cooking. Do not use cheap wine for cooking because the flavor of the dish can be altered by the quality of the wine.

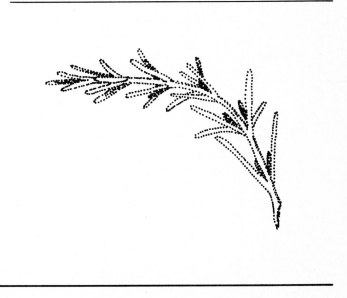

orn in Bologna, Italy's gastronomical capital, Biba Caggiano grew up cooking the food of her native Emilia-Romagna region. She met her American-born husband in Bologna where he was studying medicine. In 1960, they moved to New York. Eight years later they settled in Sacramento. Unable to find in local restaurants the northern Italian food she loved, Biba started to do much more cooking at home for her family and friends. Word of her cooking spread and she was asked to teach at a local cooking school. Soon she was also teaching in San Francisco, Los Angeles and San Diego.

In 1978, Biba was asked to do a weekly cooking segment on an evening television show called Weeknight. Since then Biba has made numerous television appearances and has been featured in articles in California newspapers.

Appetizers

*A*ntipasto means *before the pasta*. In the daily family meals, antipasti do not play a very important role. When people entertain or dine out in restaurants, antipasti become the exciting prelude to a special meal. At home, a simple antipasto generally consists of a few slices of sweet prosciutto or local salami, served with ripe cantaloupe or figs. Prosciutto and melon are the ideal antipasto because they make a light and delicate combination.

An antipasto should never be overpowering in flavor or quantity. It should only tease the palate, leaving you with a desire for more. The same rule should be applied when considering an antipasto for entertaining. An antipasto should be planned to complement the meal that will follow. Bear in mind also the wines that will be served. Don't

Menu

Mixed Cold Cuts, page 14
Tortelloni with
Ricotta Cheese & Parsley, page 52
Pork Loin Braised in Milk, page 104
Cauliflower in Batter, page 135
Strawberry Mousse, page 170
Caramino or *Pinot Noir

*California wine

serve an antipasto containing vinegar if a wine is served with it. Vinegar destroys the taste of wine.

In Italy, the best place to see antipasti displayed is in a restaurant. Italians believe that first you eat with your eyes, then with your palate. This is especially true in an Italian restaurant where antipasti are arranged on a large table or appetizer cart. One look at those mouthwatering presentations and your will power is washed away. Even in the indulgence of a special evening, don't forget the meal that will follow. Select an antipasto that will complement rather than overpower the meal.

Italian antipasti are extremely versatile. They often originate in the imagination of a good cook rather than the pages of a cookbook. Carefully selected antipasti can be served as summer buffets, late suppers or for an impromptu gathering of friends and family. An array of fresh vegetables dipped in olive oil and lemon can either start or end a meal. A cold meat dish such as Cold Veal in Tuna Fish Sauce, page 116, is equally acceptable as an antipasto or an elegant main course.

Most antipasti in this book can be prepared in very little time with a minimum of effort. Some can be prepared ahead. Feel free to improvise. Pay particular attention to the presentation and your meal will be off to a perfect start.

Baby Shrimp with Oil & Lemon

Gamberetti in Insalata

Serve with a selection of salads for a low-calorie lunch party.

2 lbs. precooked baby, bay shrimp
Juice of 2 lemons
1 teaspoon mustard
Salt and freshly ground pepper to taste
1/2 cup olive oil

3 tablespoons chopped parsley
2 garlic cloves, finely chopped
Lettuce
12 to 16 thick slices Italian bread

Pat shrimp dry with paper towels. Place shrimp in a large salad bowl. Combine lemon juice, mustard and salt and pepper in a medium bowl. Add oil, parsley and garlic; mix until blended. Taste and adjust for seasoning. Pour oil and lemon dressing over shrimp. Toss lightly until shrimp are coated with dressing. Refrigerate until ready to use. Wash and dry lettuce thoroughly. Serve shrimp at room temperature garnished with lettuce. Toast bread until golden on both sides. Serve with shrimp. Makes 6 to 8 servings.

Variation

Substitute uncooked medium shrimp for precooked bay shrimp. Boil shrimp 1 to 2 minutes. Cool, then shell and devein, page 81.

Baked Asparagus with Ham

Involtini di Asparagi con Prosciutto Cotto

Demonstrate the versatility of Italian food by serving this as an appetizer, lunch or supper.

1-1/2 lbs. asparagus
8 slices boiled ham

1/4 cup freshly grated Parmesan cheese
2 tablespoons butter

Preheat oven to 350F (175C). Butter an 11" x 7" baking dish. Cut off tough asparagus ends. Using a sharp knife or potato peeler, peel outer skin from asparagus. Tie asparagus together in 1 or 2 bunches with string or rubber bands. Pour cold salted water 2 to 3 inches deep in an asparagus cooker, tall stockpot or old coffeepot. Place asparagus upright in water. Bring water to a boil. Cover and cook over high heat 6 to 8 minutes, depending on size. Drain on paper towels; remove string or rubber bands. Divide asparagus into 4 bundles. Wrap 2 slices ham around each bundle. Arrange wrapped asparagus bundles in buttered baking dish in a single layer. Sprinkle with Parmesan cheese and dot with butter. Bake 8 to 10 minutes or until cheese is melted. Makes 4 servings.

Mozzarella & Tomatoes with Basil & Oil

Mozzarella e Pomodori al Basilico e Olio

Italian mozzarella cheese, sun-ripened tomatoes and fresh basil, this is Italian food at its best.

4 large firm tomatoes
1/2 lb. mozzarella cheese, sliced
10 to 12 fresh basil leaves

Salt and freshly ground pepper to taste
1/4 cup olive oil

Wash and dry tomatoes. Cut into slices. On a large platter, alternate mozzarella cheese and tomato slices, slightly overlapping. Place a few basil leaves between slices. Refrigerate about 15 minutes. Season with salt and pepper. Drizzle with olive oil. Makes 4 to 6 servings.

How to Make Baked Asparagus with Ham

1/Peel outer skin from asparagus.

2/Place asparagus upright in a tall stockpot.

Toasted Bread with Chicken-Liver Paste

Crostini alla Toscana

Toppings for crostini vary according to the Italian region they come from. These are from Tuscany.

1/4 cup butter
2 garlic cloves, finely chopped
1 small onion, finely chopped
10 chicken livers, finely chopped
Salt and freshly ground pepper to taste

4 fresh or dried sage leaves,
   chopped or crumbled
2 tablespoons capers, chopped
3 flat anchovy fillets, chopped
8 to 10 thick slices Italian bread

Melt butter in a small saucepan. When butter foams, add garlic and onion. Sauté over medium heat until golden. Add chicken livers. Sauté over medium heat 3 to 5 minutes or until lightly browned. Add salt and pepper, sage, capers and anchovies. Mix well; set aside. Toast bread until golden on both sides. Spread liver paste over 1 side of toasted bread, mashing it slightly as it is spread. Place on a platter. Serve warm. Makes 4 servings.

Fried Polenta with Gorgonzola Cheese

Crostini di Polenta Fritti

Prepare this dish a few hours ahead and put briefly under the broiler before serving.

Basic Polenta, page 62
6 oz. Gorgonzola cheese, room temperature
3 tablespoons butter, room temperature

1 tablespoon whipping cream
Oil for frying

Prepare Basic Polenta and let cool completely. In a small bowl, mix Gorgonzola cheese, butter and cream until blended. Set aside. Cut cooled polenta into slices 2 inches wide and 6 inches long. Pour oil about 1 inch deep in a large skillet. Heat oil until a 1-inch cube of bread turns golden almost immediately. Fry polenta slices over medium heat about 1 minute on each side or until golden. Drain on paper towels. Spread cheese mixture over hot polenta slices. Place on a warm platter. Serve immediately. Makes 6 to 8 servings.

Tomatoes Stuffed with Tuna Fish & Green Sauce

Pomodori Ripieni di Tonno e Salsa Verde

Prepare stuffing and tomatoes ahead but do not fill tomatoes until 30 minutes before serving.

1/2 cup Green Sauce, page 159
1/2 cup Mayonnaise, page 157
4 medium tomatoes
1 (7-oz.) can tuna fish in olive oil

1 to 2 tablespoons small capers
Salt and freshly ground pepper to taste
Additional capers

Prepare Green Sauce. Prepare Mayonnaise. Wash and dry tomatoes. Slice off tops. Using a small spoon, remove seeds and pulp. Drain cut-side down on paper towels 15 to 20 minutes. Drain oil from tuna. Finely chop drained tuna. Place in a medium bowl. Add Green Sauce and Mayonnaise; mix until blended. Stir in 1 to 2 tablespoons capers. Taste and adjust for seasoning. Stuff tomatoes with tuna mixture. Refrigerate 20 to 25 minutes. Garnish tomatoes with additional capers before serving. Makes 4 servings.

Prosciutto with Melon   Photo on pages 180 and 181.

Prosciutto e Melone

Be sure to use top-quality prosciutto and juicy, sweet melons.

2 medium cantaloupes
12 slices prosciutto, page 6

Cut each cantaloupe into 6 slices. Remove rind. Wrap 1 slice prosciutto around each cantaloupe slice. Place on a large platter. Serve at room temperature. Makes 6 servings.

Variation

Prosciutto with Figs (Prosciutto e Fichi): Substitute 12 figs for cantaloupes.

Russian Salad

Insalata Russa

A delicious Italian salad that somehow inherited a foreign name.

1-1/4 cups Mayonnaise, page 157	**3 tablespoons capers**
1 cup frozen peas, thawed	**Salt and freshly ground pepper to taste**
1/4 lb. string beans	**3 tablespoons olive oil**
2 zucchini	**1 or 2 tablespoons red wine vinegar**
2 carrots	**8 to 10 black olives**
2 medium potatoes	**2 or 3 hard-cooked eggs, sliced**

Prepare Mayonnaise. Fill a small saucepan half full with water. Add peas. Cook 20 to 30 seconds over high heat. Drain and set aside. Trim and wash string beans and zucchini. Fill a large saucepan two-thirds full with salted water. Bring water to a boil. Add string beans, zucchini, carrots and potatoes. Cook 5 to 8 minutes over high heat. Test string beans, zucchini and carrots. Remove when tender but firm. Drain on paper towels. Cook potatoes 10 to 15 minutes longer or until tender but firm. Peel while hot. Let vegetables cool. Finely dice cooled vegetables. Place diced vegetables in a large bowl. Add 2 tablespoons capers and peas. Season with salt and pepper. Add oil and vinegar; mix until blended. Taste and adjust salad for seasoning. Gently mix in 1 cup Mayonnaise. Place salad on a large round dish. Pile neatly in a mound, pressing it gently with your hands. Pour remaining Mayonnaise over salad mound. Cover and refrigerate several hours or overnight. Before serving, garnish top of mound with remaining capers and olives. Arrange slices of hard-cooked eggs around base of salad. Serve slightly chilled. Makes 6 to 8 servings.

Variation

Tomatoes Stuffed with Russian Salad (Pomodori Ripieni di Insalata Russa): Slice off tops from 6 medium tomatoes. Using a small spoon, remove seeds and pulp. Drain cut-side down on paper towels 15 to 20 minutes. Stuff with Russian Salad. Makes 6 servings.

Mixed Cold Cuts

Antipasto all'Italiana

This can probably be considered Italy's national antipasto.

**4 to 6 oz. prosciutto, page 6,
  thinly sliced**
4 to 6 oz. coppa, thinly sliced
4 to 6 oz. boiled ham, thinly sliced
4 to 6 oz. mortadella, thinly sliced
4 to 6 oz. salami, thinly sliced

4 to 6 oz. sopressata, thinly sliced
Radishes
Black olives
Artichoke hearts
Green onions

Arrange cold cuts attractively on a large platter. Garnish with radishes, black olives, artichoke hearts and green onions. Makes 4 to 6 servings.

Hot Anchovy Dip

Bagna Caôda

This classic Piedmont dish is typical of the region's robust cuisine.

2 fennels
2 celery hearts
2 large, red or green sweet peppers
1 or 2 bunches radishes, trimmed
1/2 lb. small asparagus

1/4 cup butter
3/4 cup olive oil
6 garlic cloves, finely chopped
8 flat anchovy fillets, chopped
Salt and freshly ground pepper, if desired

Cut off long stalks and bruised leaves from fennels. Slice ends off bulbous bases. Wash and dry fennels. Cut into quarters, then horizontally into thick slices. Wash and dry celery hearts, peppers, radishes and asparagus. Slice celery hearts in half lengthwise. Slice peppers into quarters and remove seeds. Cut off tough asparagus ends. Using a sharp knife or potato peeler, peel outer skin. Arrange vegetables on a large platter. Melt butter with oil in a small earthenware pot or small saucepan. When butter foams, add garlic. Sauté over medium heat. When garlic begins to color, add anchovies. Reduce heat to very low. Stir until anchovies have almost dissolved. Season sparingly with salt and pepper, if desired. Keep dip warm at the table over a burner or on a warming tray. Serve with prepared vegetables. Makes 4 servings.

Variation

Vegetables with Olive Oil Dip (Verdure in Pinzimonio): Prepare fresh vegetables. Combine 1 cup olive oil, 2 tablespoons salt and pepper to taste in a small bowl. Spoon dressing into 4 small bowls and place at each table setting.

Mixed Cold Cuts and Roasted Peppers, page 16

Roasted Peppers   Photo on page 15.

Peperoni Arrostiti

As a marvelous appetizer, or an incomparable salad, sweet peppers have never tasted so good.

**8 medium, red, yellow or
   green sweet peppers**
1/2 cup olive oil
6 flat anchovy fillets, mashed

**3 tablespoons chopped parsley or
   fresh basil**
4 garlic cloves, finely chopped
Salt and freshly ground pepper to taste

Roast peppers over an open flame or under the broiler until skin is dark brown and blistered. Place peppers in a large plastic or brown paper bag and set aside 5 to 10 minutes. Peel peppers. Cut in half and remove pith and seeds. Cut peeled peppers into large strips. Pat dry with paper towels. Arrange peppers slightly overlapping on a medium platter. In a small bowl, combine oil, anchovies, parsley or basil, garlic and salt and pepper. Taste and adjust for seasoning. Spoon anchovy dressing over peppers. Refrigerate several hours or overnight. Serve at room temperature. Makes 6 to 8 servings.

Garlic Bread

Fettunta

Originally a poor man's staple, Fettunta is served today in some of the best Tuscan restaurants.

8 to 10 thick slices Italian bread
4 garlic cloves, cut in half

1/2 cup olive oil
Salt and freshly ground pepper to taste

Toast bread until golden on both sides. Rub toasted bread with cut garlic on both sides. Heat oil in a small saucepan. Drizzle hot oil over toasted bread. Season with salt and pepper. Place bread on a warm platter. Serve immediately. Makes 4 servings.

Best-quality olive oil is an essential part of Garlic Bread.

How to Make Roasted Peppers

1/Peel blistered peppers.

2/Cut peeled peppers into large strips.

Fried Marinated Sardines

Sardine in Carpione

A classic dish with an unusually spicy flavor—from the Veneto region.

1 lb. small fresh sardines, cleaned
1/2 cup all-purpose flour
3/4 cup vegetable oil
Salt and freshly ground pepper to taste

3 or 4 fresh or dried bay leaves
2 medium onions, thinly sliced
1/3 cup white wine vinegar

Cut heads off sardines. Wash and dry fish thoroughly. Spread flour on aluminum foil. Coat sardines lightly with flour. Heat 1/2 cup oil in a medium skillet. Cook sardines over medium heat 2 to 3 minutes on each side or until golden. Drain on paper towels. Season with salt and pepper. Place drained sardines in a shallow dish. Arrange bay leaves on top; set aside. Heat remaining oil in another medium skillet. Add onions. Sauté over medium heat until pale yellow. Add vinegar. Cook and stir 30 to 50 seconds. Pour onion mixture over sardines. Cover and refrigerate 24 hours. Serve at room temperature. Makes 4 servings.

Soups

Soup is not the first item that comes to mind when you think about Italian food, but Italy has an outstanding selection of soups. Unfortunately, they have been upstaged by pasta both at home and abroad. Soup is always the first course and it is into the first course that Italians have poured their hearts and traditions. The one Italian soup that non-Italians are familiar with is *Minestrone*. All too often this turns out to be a watery soup with pieces of vegetables and a few beans swimming about aimlessly in too much liquid. A soup in Italy takes on the characteristics of the region it comes from and embodies its traditions.

When I was growing up in Bologna, there was never any question of how to serve *tortellini*. In the classic Bolognese tradition, tortellini were always served in a rich broth. But today most people associate tortellini only with a cream sauce. Although Emilia-Romagna is the home of the very best *lasagne*, *tortellini* and *tagliatelle*, the traditional Sunday dinner in my family was always soup. The aroma of simmering broth filled the house by 8 a.m. Each Sunday a different kind of pasta would be cooked in the broth.

Menu

Onion Soup Italian-Style, page 27
Filet Mignons with Brandy,
Cream & Peppercorns, page 122
Baked Fennel with Butter
& Cheese, page 135
Italian Rum Cake, page 182
Barolo or *Cabernet Sauvignon

*California wine

In some regions, soups are even more popular than pasta. Veneto, for example, boasts some of the best soups in Italy. Thick vegetable and bean soups are especially notable. Italian soups can be delicate and elegant, like Tortellini in Broth. The lentil and bean soups, on the other hand, are substantial and filling. All these soups have one thing in common: a good broth. To produce a good soup, one must first produce a good broth. Broth is also a very important ingredient in other kinds of Italian cooking. With a good broth you can produce a sensational soup or add to meat juices to make a flavorful sauce. A good broth is also a key ingredient when making a perfect *risotto*.

In this chapter you will find recipes for a basic meat and chicken broth. Meat Broth is easy and inexpensive to make and can be used for soups and other cooking. Chicken Broth makes a good base for light soups and is ideal for risotto. Mixed Boiled Meats, page 120, produces an especially good broth because of the quality of meats used.

For a fine broth, remember these basic rules: Cooking should be done over very low heat. The broth should not boil, but should simmer very gently for 2-1/2 to 3-1/2 hours. This allows all the goodness and flavor of the meat and bones to be extracted. During the first few minutes of cooking, the surface foam should be skimmed off frequently. Seasoning should be done at the end because the liquid will reduce during cooking, concentrating the flavor.

We all have childhood memories that give us comfort and happiness. To me it is the memory of my mother in the kitchen preparing the Sunday dinner. Her soup would bring a glow to everyone's cheeks and fill us with a feeling of well-being.

Good food is a labor of love. How lucky we are not only to receive it but also to pass it on to our family and friends.

Meat Broth

Brodo di Carne

Keep a supply of this delicious broth in your freezer for soups and other cooking.

3 to 3-1/2 lbs. bones and meat scraps
   from beef, chicken, veal
1/2 cup loosely packed parsley
2 carrots, chopped
2 celery stalks, chopped

1 medium onion, sliced
2 medium tomatoes, chopped, or
   1 tablespoon tomato paste
4 quarts water
1 tablespoon salt

Place all ingredients except salt in a large stockpot. Cover and bring to a boil. Reduce heat to very low. Simmer covered 2-1/2 to 3 hours, skimming surface foam occasionally with a slotted spoon. Add salt. Strain broth and use. Cool broth completely before freezing. Makes 2 to 2-1/2 quarts of broth.

Chicken Broth

Brodo di Gallina

In Italy, hens are used to give the broth a distinct flavor.

1 (2- to 3-lb.) chicken hen	2 medium tomatoes, chopped, or
1 to 1-1/2 lbs. chicken bones and scraps	1 tablespoon tomato paste
2 celery stalks, chopped	4 quarts water
1 medium onion, sliced	1 tablespoon salt

Place all ingredients except salt in a large stockpot. Cover and bring to a boil. Reduce heat to very low. Simmer covered 1 to 1-1/2 hours, skimming surface foam occasionally with a slotted spoon. Add salt. Strain broth and use. Cool broth completely before freezing. Makes 2 to 2-1/2 quarts of broth.

Lentil Soup

Zuppa di Lenticchie

The flavor of this nutritious soup improves if made one or two days ahead.

2 cups lentils	1/4 cup olive oil
4 cups Meat Broth, page 19, or	1 medium onion, finely chopped
3 cups canned beef broth	2 tablespoons chopped parsley
6 to 8 cups water	2 garlic cloves, chopped
2 celery stalks, finely chopped	1/4 lb. pancetta, page 6, chopped
2 carrots, finely chopped	Salt and freshly ground pepper to taste
1 cup canned crushed Italian-style or	8 to 10 thick slices Italian bread
whole tomatoes	1 cup freshly grated Parmesan cheese

Place lentils in a large bowl. Add enough cold water to cover and let stand overnight. Discard any lentils that float to the surface. Drain and rinse lentils thoroughly. Prepare Meat Broth. Place lentils in a large saucepan. Add water, broth, celery and carrots. Cover and bring to a boil. Reduce heat. Simmer 50 to 60 minutes, stirring occasionally. Press tomatoes through a food mill or sieve, page 161, to remove seeds. Heat oil in a small saucepan. Add onion, parsley and garlic. Sauté over medium heat 2 to 3 minutes. Add pancetta. Sauté 2 to 3 minutes or until pancetta is lightly browned. Add tomato pulp. Season with salt and pepper. Reduce heat. Cook uncovered 15 to 20 minutes. With a slotted spoon, place a third of lentil mixture in a blender or food processor. Process until smooth. Return to saucepan. Add tomato mixture. Simmer uncovered 10 minutes. Taste and adjust for seasoning. Toast bread until golden on both sides. Place 1 slice toasted bread in each soup bowl. Sprinkle generously with Parmesan cheese. Ladle soup into bowls. Serve hot or at room temperature. Makes 8 to 10 servings.

Vegetable Soup

Minestrone di Verdura

There are as many versions of vegetable soup in Italy as there are cooks.

8 cups Chicken Broth, opposite, or
    4 cups canned chicken broth and
    4 cups water
1/3 cup olive oil
1/4 cup chopped parsley
4 garlic cloves, chopped
1/4 lb. pancetta, page 6, finely chopped
3 cups shredded cabbage
1 medium onion, finely chopped
2 carrots, finely chopped

1 celery stalk, finely chopped
1 potato, peeled, finely chopped
2 zucchini, finely chopped
1 large tomato, chopped
1/4 lb. mushrooms, finely chopped
1/4 lb. string beans, finely chopped
3 or 4 pieces prosciutto rind, page 6,
    or 1 smoked ham shank
Salt and freshly ground pepper to taste
1/2 cup freshly grated Parmesan cheese

Prepare Chicken Broth. Heat oil in a large saucepan. Add parsley and garlic. Sauté over medium heat. Before garlic changes color, add pancetta. Sauté until lightly browned. Stir in cabbage. Cover and cook 1 to 2 minutes. Add remaining vegetables to saucepan. Cover and cook about 5 minutes. Add broth and water, if using, and prosciutto rind or ham shank. Cover and reduce heat. Simmer 40 to 50 minutes. Remove half the vegetables with a slotted spoon. Place in a blender or food processor and process until smooth. Return to saucepan. Season with salt and pepper. Serve hot with Parmesan cheese. Makes 8 to 10 servings.

Variation

Toast about 20 thick slices Italian bread. Place 2 slices in each soup bowl and sprinkle generously with Parmesan cheese. Ladle soup into bowls. Serve with additional Parmesan cheese.

You can transform a vegetable soup into a cream of vegetable soup. Puree the vegetables in a food processor or blender and stir in some cream.

Parmesan Cheese, Breadcrumb & Nutmeg Soup

Passatelli in Brodo

A delicious and unique soup from the Emilia-Romagna region.

10 to 12 cups broth from
   Mixed Boiled Meats, page 120, or
   Meat Broth, page 19
3/4 cup freshly grated Parmesan cheese

1/2 cup fine, dry unflavored breadcrumbs
1/2 teaspoon freshly grated nutmeg
2 large eggs
Additional Parmesan cheese

Prepare Meat Broth. On a pastry board or in a large bowl, combine 3/4 cup Parmesan cheese, breadcrumbs and nutmeg. Mix well. Add eggs. Mix ingredients thoroughly and work into a ball. Dough should be smooth and pliable. Bring broth to a boil in a large saucepan. Put dough into a ricer or food mill and rice directly into broth. Reduce heat. Simmer 1 to 2 minutes. Serve hot with Parmesan cheese. Makes 6 to 8 servings.

Rice & Pea Soup

Risi e Bisi

This classic Venetian soup should be thick enough to eat with a fork.

8 cups Meat Broth, page 19
1/4 cup butter
1 tablespoon olive oil
1 small onion, chopped
1/4 lb. pancetta, page 6, chopped
2 tablespoons chopped parsley

2-1/2 cups fresh peas or frozen peas,
   thawed
2 cups arborio rice, page 6
1/3 cup freshly grated Parmesan cheese
Additional Parmesan cheese

Prepare Meat Broth. Melt 2 tablespoons butter with oil in a medium saucepan. When butter foams, add onion, pancetta and parsley. Sauté over medium heat until pancetta is lightly browned. Add peas and 1/3 cup broth. Cook 2 to 3 minutes; set aside. Bring remaining broth to a boil in a large saucepan. Add rice. Cook uncovered over high heat 8 to 10 minutes, stirring occasionally. Add onion mixture. Cook 10 to 15 minutes or until rice is tender but firm to the bite. Stir in remaining butter and 1/3 cup Parmesan cheese. Serve hot with additional Parmesan cheese. Makes 6 to 8 servings.

How to Make Parmesan Cheese, Breadcrumb & Nutmeg Soup

1/Add eggs to breadcrumb mixture.

2/Work dough into a ball.

3/Press dough through ricer into broth.

4/Serve hot soup with Parmesan cheese.

Tortellini in Broth

Tortellini in Brodo

On Sunday mornings our house was filled with the aroma of simmering broth.

**10 to 12 cups broth from
  Mixed Boiled Meats, page 120,
  or Meat Broth, page 19**

**Tortellini, page 50
1 cup freshly grated Parmesan cheese**

Prepare Meat Broth. Prepare and fill tortellini. Bring broth to a boil in a large saucepan. Add tortellini. Boil gently until tortellini are tender but firm to the bite, page 29. Serve hot with Parmesan cheese. Makes 6 to 8 servings.

My Mother's Bean Soup

Zuppa di Fagioli alla Maniera di mia Madre

There are certain childhood dishes that cannot be forgotten. For me, this hearty soup is one of them.

**2 cups dried pinto beans
4 cups Meat Broth, page 19, or
  3 cups canned beef broth
6 to 8 cups water
1 large potato, peeled, halved
1 carrot, halved
1 celery stalk, halved
2 to 3 slices prosciutto rind, page 6,
  or salt pork
1 cup canned crushed Italian-style or
  whole tomatoes**

**1/4 cup olive oil
3 tablespoons chopped parsley
2 garlic cloves, chopped
1 small onion, chopped
1/4 lb. pancetta, page 6, chopped
Salt and freshly ground pepper to taste
8 to 10 thick slices Italian bread
1 cup freshly grated Parmesan cheese**

Place beans in a large bowl. Add enough cold water to cover and let stand overnight. Drain and rinse beans thoroughly. Prepare Meat Broth. Place beans in a large saucepan. Add water, broth, potato, carrot, celery and prosciutto rind or salt pork. Cover and bring to a boil. Reduce heat. Simmer 50 to 60 minutes, stirring occasionally. Press tomatoes through a food mill or sieve, page 161, to remove seeds. Heat oil in a medium saucepan. Add parsley, garlic and onion. Sauté over medium heat 2 to 3 minutes. Add pancetta. Sauté until pancetta is lightly browned. Stir in tomato pulp and season with salt and pepper. Reduce heat. Cook uncovered 15 to 20 minutes. With a slotted spoon, place potato, carrot, celery and half the beans in a blender or food processor. Process until smooth. Return to saucepan. Add tomato mixture. Simmer uncovered 10 minutes. Taste and adjust for seasoning. Toast bread until golden on both sides. Place 1 slice toasted bread in each soup bowl. Sprinkle generously with Parmesan cheese. Ladle soup into bowls. Makes 8 to 10 servings.

Tortellini in Broth

Bean Soup Veneto-Style

Pasta e Fagioli alla Veneta

The Veneto region is famous for its marvelous bean soups.

2 cups dried pinto beans
4 cups Meat Broth, page 19, or
   3 cups canned beef broth
6 to 8 cups water
6 tablespoons olive oil
2 slices prosciutto rind, page 6, or
   salt pork
1 carrot, chopped
1 celery stalk, chopped
1 medium onion, chopped
1 sprig fresh rosemary or
   1 teaspoon dried rosemary

2 tablespoons chopped parsley
2 garlic cloves, chopped
1 tablespoon all-purpose flour
2 tablespoons tomato paste
Salt and freshly ground pepper to taste
1/4 lb. small elbow macaroni, ditalini or
   arborio rice, page 6
1/3 cup freshly grated Parmesan cheese
Additional Parmesan cheese

Place beans in a large bowl. Add enough cold water to cover and let stand overnight. Drain and rinse beans thoroughly. Prepare Meat Broth. Place beans in a large saucepan. Add water, broth, 2 tablespoons oil, prosciutto rind or salt pork, carrot, celery and onion. Cover and bring to a boil. Reduce heat. Simmer 50 to 60 minutes, stirring occasionally. Heat 3 tablespoons oil in a small saucepan. Add rosemary. Cook over medium heat until lightly browned. Discard rosemary. Add parsley and garlic; sauté. When garlic changes color, stir in flour. Cook and stir about 1 minute. Remove 1 cup cooking liquid from bean mixture. Stir in tomato paste. Stir into flour mixture. Season with salt and pepper. Cook 5 to 10 minutes, stirring frequently. Add to bean mixture. With a slotted spoon, place a third of bean mixture in a blender or food processor. Process until smooth. Return to saucepan. Bring soup to a boil. Add pasta or rice and cook over high heat 8 to 10 minutes. Stir several times during cooking. Taste and adjust for seasoning. Stir 1 tablespoon oil and 1/3 cup Parmesan cheese into soup. Serve hot with additional Parmesan cheese. Makes 8 to 10 servings.

Bread Soup Parma-Style

Pancotto

This thick traditional soup from Parma proves that nothing goes to waste in an Italian kitchen.

8 to 10 cups Meat Broth, page 19
8 slices stale Italian bread
Salt and freshly ground pepper to taste
3 tablespoons butter
2 tablespoons olive oil

2 fresh or dried sage leaves,
   chopped or crumbled
1/3 cup freshly grated Parmesan cheese
Additional Parmesan cheese

Prepare Meat Broth. Put 8 cups broth and bread into a medium saucepan. Bring to a boil. Reduce heat. Cook uncovered over medium heat 20 to 30 minutes, stirring occasionally. If soup looks too dry during cooking, add 1 to 2 cups broth. Season with salt and pepper. Add butter, oil and sage. Cook 5 minutes longer. Stir in 1/3 cup Parmesan cheese. Taste and adjust for seasoning. Serve hot or at room temperature with additional Parmesan cheese. Makes 4 servings.

Cream of Potato & Leek Soup

Crema di Patate e Porri

Leeks are closely related to onions but have a flavor all their own.

6 to 8 cups Meat Broth, page 19
2 lbs. potatoes
1 lb. leeks
2 egg yolks
1/2 cup whipping cream

1 tablespoon chopped parsley
Salt and freshly ground pepper to taste
1/2 cup freshly grated Parmesan cheese
Toasted bread

Prepare Meat Broth. Peel and chop potatoes. Trim ends and tough outside leaves from leeks. Cut leeks lengthwise through to center. Wash under cold running water, pulling layers apart so grit is removed. Slice into rounds. Put potatoes and leeks into a medium saucepan. Add enough broth to cover. Cook uncovered over medium heat until vegetables are tender. With a slotted spoon, place vegetables in a blender or food processor. Process until smooth. Return puree to broth. Bring mixture to a boil. Remove from heat. Beat together egg yolks and cream in a small bowl. Quickly beat egg yolk mixture into hot soup. Stir in parsley. Season with salt and pepper. Serve hot with Parmesan cheese and toasted bread. Makes 6 servings.

Onion Soup Italian-Style

Zuppa di Cipolle all'Italiana

Homemade Meat Broth, page 19, and top-quality Parmesan cheese are vital to the success of this soup.

10 to 12 cups Meat Broth, page 19
6 tablespoons butter
8 large onions, thinly sliced
1/3 cup brandy

1/2 cup all-purpose flour
12 thick slices Italian bread
1 to 1-1/2 cups freshly grated
    Parmesan cheese

Prepare Meat Broth. Simmer broth in a large saucepan. Melt butter in another large saucepan. When butter foams, add onions. Sauté over medium heat until pale yellow. Stir in brandy. When brandy is three-quarters evaporated, stir in flour. Reduce heat to medium-low. Cook 1 to 2 minutes, stirring constantly. Gradually stir in hot broth. Season with salt and pepper. Cover and simmer 30 to 40 minutes. Preheat oven to 350F (175C). Toast bread until golden on both sides. Place 2 slices toasted bread in each of 6 ovenproof soup bowls. Add 1 to 2 tablespoons Parmesan cheese. Ladle soup into bowls. Sprinkle each serving with a generous tablespoon Parmesan cheese. Bake 10 to 12 minutes. Place briefly under preheated broiler for a golden crust. Serve immediately. Makes 6 servings.

Pasta

The general belief that Marco Polo introduced pasta from China is not true. Marco Polo left for China in 1271 and returned in 1295. During that long journey he wrote that he had found "noodles like ours." Documents dated during the years Marco Polo was in China show that *lasagne, tortellini* and *ravioli* were already known to Italians.

Food historians go a step further and trace the origins of pasta to the Roman Empire. Whatever its origins, pasta has retained its dominance in Italian cuisine. Pasta is a national institution.

Let me start by explaining a few important points about pasta and pasta-making. First I will try to dispel the notion that pasta is fattening. Pasta, like most other food, is fattening if eaten in large amounts. In Italy, pasta is eaten daily yet few grossly overweight people are seen. Pasta is an economical and satisfying food. Two ounces of pasta with a moderate amount of sauce will generally satisfy your hunger. That amount of pasta without the sauce has only 200 calories. The rest of the world can finally discover what Italians have known for centuries!

Equipment

Pasta machines of every kind have been introduced into the market. These have made pasta-making easier.

There are two types of pasta machines for the home. One is hand-cranked and the other is electric. The electric model is faster and its textured rollers give a better texture to the pasta. It is also more expensive. The hand-cranked machine has steel rollers and will produce a slightly more slippery pasta. Which one you choose will depend on your needs and budget.

Both types are easy to operate and work on the same principle. The main part of the machine is for kneading and rolling the dough. It also has two sets of cutters. The broad cutter will produce regular noodles, the narrow cutter will produce the thinner *tagliarini*.

The best surface for kneading pasta is wood. The warmth and grain of wood will give your dough a special elasticity, texture and consistency. Formica can also be used. Marble is not used because its cold surface will produce a tight, less-elastic dough.

Ingredients

Use unbleached all-purpose flour whenever possible. This is the flour that is most like Italian flour. With a few exceptions, semolina flour, made from durum wheat, is not used in northern Italy to make homemade pasta. It is almost always used in factory-made pasta.

Use large eggs brought to room temperature. If you can find eggs with a really orange yolk, your pasta will have the golden color that egg pasta should have. In some parts of Italy, a drop of oil and a pinch of salt are added to the dough. In Emilia-Romagna we use only flour and eggs.

Cutting, Storing & Cooking Noodles

Roll pasta dough into thin sheets using a machine. Dry pasta sheets 10 to 15 minutes. Put through the widest cutting blade of the pasta machine. Arrange cut noodles in soft bundles to dry. If you plan to store noodles, let them dry at least 24 hours. At this point noodles are brittle. Place them gently in plastic bags or large jars. Seal tightly and store at room temperature. They will keep well for two to three weeks.

To cook fresh noodles, fill a very large saucepan two-thirds full with salted water. Bring the water to a boil. Add pasta. Bring water back to a boil. Cook pasta, uncovered, for 5 to 20 seconds after the water returns to a boil. Do not overcook pasta. It should always be *al dente*, tender but firm to the bite. Pasta that is more than a day old will need longer cooking. Follow this rule: The fresher the pasta, the shorter the cooking time.

Cutting, Storing & Cooking Stuffed Pasta

For stuffed pasta, such as *tortellini* and *agnolotti*, each sheet of dough must be cut and stuffed immediately so the moistness of the dough can give a tight seal. Stuffed pasta should not be made more than one or two days ahead of cooking time. Many stuffings are very moist and if left to stand will make the dough sticky. Specific instructions on cutting and stuffing pasta are given with recipes. The principle for cooking stuffed pasta is the same as that for noodles: The fresher the pasta, the shorter the cooking time.

Dried Pasta

In Italy, the shapes and sizes of factory-made pasta are innumerable. Outside Italy there is less choice but *spaghetti*, *macaroni* and noodles are available everywhere. To select a good-quality dried pasta, read the label. It should say "100% semolina flour." Another indication of a good pasta is that it should almost double in volume when it is cooked al dente. The cooking time of dried pasta varies slightly according to the brand you choose. As a general rule, 10 minutes will give you pasta that is al dente.

Green Lasagne Bologna-Style, page 49
Veal Scaloppine with Marsala
Wine, page 112
Peas with Prosciutto, page 136
Hot Zabaglione, page 177
Valpolicella-Valpantena or *Zinfandel

*California wine

Basic Egg Pasta Dough

Pasta all'Uovo

Altitude, humidity and the size of the eggs will influence the amount of flour needed to make pasta.

Use these ingredients	To Make		
	3 to 4 servings	5 to 6 servings	7 to 8 servings
all-purpose flour	2-1/4 cups	3 cups	4-1/2 cups
eggs	3	4	6

Put flour on a pastry board and make a well in the center. Break eggs into well; beat with a fork. Draw some flour from inner rim of well over eggs, beating constantly. Keep adding flour a little at a time until you have a soft dough. Put dough aside. With a pastry scraper, remove bits and pieces of dough attached to board. Lightly flour board and your hands. Knead dough 10 to 12 minutes, adding flour a little at a time until dough is smooth and pliable. Insert a finger into center of dough. If it comes out almost dry, dough is ready for pasta machine. If dough is sticky, knead it a little longer adding more flour. Set rollers of pasta machine at their widest opening. Cut an egg-size piece from dough. Wrap remaining dough in a cloth towel to prevent it from drying. Flatten small piece of dough, dust with flour and fold in half. Run it through pasta machine. Repeat this step 5 to 8 times or until dough is smooth and not sticky. Change notch of pasta machine to the next setting and run dough through once without folding it. Keep changing setting and working pasta sheet through machine until pasta reaches desired thickness. A good thickness for general use is about 1/16 inch. Sprinkle dough with flour between rollings if it is sticky.

Basic Spinach Pasta Dough

Pasta Verde

Once you have tasted homemade pasta, no substitute will do!

Use these ingredients	To Make		
	3 to 4 servings	5 to 6 servings	7 to 8 servings
frozen spinach	1/3 (10-oz.) pkg.	1/2 (10-oz.) pkg.	2/3 (10-oz.) pkg.
all-purpose flour	2 cups	3 cups	4 cups
eggs	2	3	4

Cook spinach according to package instructions. Drain thoroughly. Squeeze spinach to remove as much moisture as possible. Chop spinach very fine. Put flour on a pastry board and make a well in the center. Break eggs into well; beat with a fork. Add chopped spinach and beat to combine. Continue as for Basic Egg Pasta Dough, above.

How to Make Basic Egg Pasta Dough

1/Mix flour from inner rim of well with eggs.

2/Knead dough until smooth and pliable.

3/Fold dough in half each time before putting it through pasta machine.

4/Keep putting dough through machine until dough reaches desired thickness.

Tagliatelle with Walnut Sauce

Tagliatelle con le Noci

A simple dish with a delightful flavor.

**Basic Egg Pasta Dough, page 30, made with
  2-1/4 cups all-purpose flour**

**Walnut Sauce, see below
1/2 cup freshly grated Parmesan cheese**

Walnut Sauce:
**3/4 cup whole walnuts
3 tablespoons butter
1/4 cup olive oil
3 to 4 tablespoons milk**

**2 to 3 tablespoons ricotta cheese
2 tablespoons chopped parsley
Salt and freshly ground pepper to taste**

Prepare noodles, page 29, from Basic Egg Pasta Dough, page 30. Prepare Walnut Sauce and let stand at room temperature. Fill a very large saucepan two-thirds full with salted water. Bring water to a boil. Add noodles. Bring water back to a boil and cook noodles uncovered until tender but firm to the bite, page 29. Drain noodles and place in a warm deep dish or bowl. Add Walnut Sauce and toss gently until mixed. Serve immediately with Parmesan cheese. Makes 4 servings.

Walnut Sauce:
Put walnuts in a blender or food processor and process until finely chopped. Add butter, oil, milk, ricotta cheese and parsley. Blend at high speed to a thin sauce. Season with salt and pepper.

Tagliatelle with Peas & Bacon

Tagliatelle con Piselli e Pancetta

A good example of uncomplicated cooking.

**Basic Egg Pasta Dough, page 30, made with
  2-1/4 cups all-purpose flour
1 cup Plain Tomato Sauce, page 161
3 tablespoons butter
1/4 lb. pancetta, page 6, cut into
  4 slices and diced**

**3/4 cup whipping cream
1 cup frozen peas, thawed
Salt and freshly ground pepper to taste
1/4 cup freshly grated Parmesan cheese
Additional Parmesan cheese**

Prepare noodles, page 29, from Basic Egg Pasta Dough, page 30. Prepare Plain Tomato Sauce. Melt butter in a large skillet. When butter foams, add pancetta. Sauté over medium heat until lightly colored. Add tomato sauce, cream and peas. Stir over low heat until sauce has a medium-thick consistency, 3 to 4 minutes. Season with salt and pepper. Fill a very large saucepan two-thirds full with salted water. Bring water to a boil. Add noodles. Bring water back to a boil and cook noodles uncovered until tender but firm to the bite, page 29. Drain noodles and place in skillet with sauce. Add 1/4 cup Parmesan cheese. Toss noodles and sauce over medium heat until sauce coats noodles, 20 to 30 seconds. Serve immediately with additional Parmesan cheese. Makes 4 to 6 servings.

Green Tagliatelle with Bacon Sauce

Tagliatelle Verdi alla Pancetta

The sauce can also be served over spaghetti and macaroni.

Basic Spinach Pasta Dough, page 30,
 made with 2 cups all-purpose flour
1/4 cup olive oil
1 medium onion, finely chopped
1/4 lb. pancetta, page 6,
 cut into 4 slices and diced

1 (28-oz.) can crushed Italian-style or
 whole tomatoes
Salt and freshly ground pepper to taste
1/2 cup freshly grated Parmesan cheese

Prepare noodles, page 29, from Basic Spinach Pasta Dough, page 30. Heat oil in a medium saucepan. Add onion and sauté over medium heat until pale yellow. Add pancetta and sauté until lightly colored. Press tomatoes through a food mill or sieve, page 161, to remove seeds. Stir tomato pulp into saucepan. Simmer uncovered 25 to 30 minutes or until sauce reduces to a medium-thick consistency. Season with salt and pepper. Fill a very large saucepan two-thirds full with salted water. Bring water to a boil. Add noodles. Bring water back to a boil and cook noodles uncovered until tender but firm to the bite, page 29. Drain noodles and place in a warm deep dish or bowl. Add sauce and toss gently until mixed. Serve immediately with Parmesan cheese. Makes 4 to 6 servings.

Classic Method for Making Pasta Dough

Prepare dough as directed on page 30. Place dough on a lightly floured surface. Flatten ball of dough with a rolling pin or the palms of your hands. The ideal rolling pin should be 32 inches long and 1-1/2 inches in diameter. Roll out dough, starting from center and moving toward edges. Rotate dough slightly and roll out again from center toward edges. Repeat several times. Dough should be rolled into a wide circle. Dust surface lightly if sticking. To roll out pasta to an even thinness, wrap the far edge of pasta sheet around rolling pin. Roll less than half pasta sheet toward you. With the palms of your hands, gently press against center of rolling pin. Roll pin forward while the palms of your hands move toward ends of rolling pin. With this motion, pasta will be stretched forward as well as sideways. Rotate sheet of pasta slightly and repeat the motion. Dust lightly with flour if dough is sticky. Repeat this step until dough is thin and almost transparent. Try to work as quickly as possible to avoid dough drying.

For stuffed pasta, cut into desired shapes and stuff immediately. For noodles, let pasta circle dry on a wooden surface or tablecloth 15 to 20 minutes. Fold pasta loosely into a flat roll, not wider than 3 inches. With a large sharp knife, cut pasta into desired width. Open out noodles. Place in soft bundles on a wooden surface or tablecloth. Dry noodles 10 to 15 minutes longer before cooking. Dry completely for 24 hours if you intend to store them.

Green Tagliatelle with Salmon Sauce

Tagliatelle Verdi al Salmone

A small amount of salmon goes a long way in this dish.

Basic Spinach Pasta Dough, page 30,
  made with 2 cups all-purpose flour
1-1/2 cups Plain Tomato Sauce, page 161
1/4 cup butter
1/4 lb. prosciutto, page 6, diced

1/2 lb. fresh salmon fillet,
  cut in very small pieces
1/2 cup whipping cream
Salt and freshly ground pepper to taste

Prepare noodles, page 29, from Basic Spinach Pasta Dough, page 30. Prepare Plain Tomato Sauce. Melt butter in a large skillet. When butter foams, add prosciutto and salmon. Stir over medium heat 2 to 3 minutes. If salmon sticks together, break it apart with a fork. Stir in tomato sauce and cream. Season with salt and pepper. Simmer uncovered 8 to 10 minutes. Fill a very large saucepan two-thirds full with salted water. Bring water to a boil. Add noodles. Bring water back to a boil and cook noodles uncovered until tender but firm to the bite, page 29. Drain noodles and place in skillet with sauce. Toss noodles and sauce over medium heat until sauce coats noodles, 20 to 30 seconds. Serve immediately. Makes 4 servings.

Green & Yellow Tagliatelle with Mushroom Sauce

Tagliatelle Verdi e Gialle con Salsa di Funghi

I cooked this beautiful dish for a dinner party and I received applause. What a reward!

Basic Spinach Pasta Dough, page 30,
  made with 2 cups all-purpose flour
Basic Egg Pasta Dough, page 30, made with
  2-1/4 cups all-purpose flour
1 lb. small white mushrooms
1/4 cup butter

1 cup whipping cream
2 tablespoons chopped parsley
Salt and freshly ground pepper to taste
1/3 cup freshly grated Parmesan cheese
Additional Parmesan cheese

Prepare noodles, page 29, from Basic Spinach Pasta Dough and Basic Egg Pasta Dough, page 30. Wash and dry mushrooms thoroughly and slice thin. Melt butter in a large skillet. When butter foams, add mushrooms. Sauté over high heat until lightly colored. Stir in cream, parsley and salt and pepper. Simmer 2 to 3 minutes or until cream begins to thicken. Fill a very large saucepan two-thirds full with salted water. Bring water to a boil. Add noodles. Bring water back to a boil and cook noodles uncovered until tender but firm to the bite, page 29. Drain noodles and place in skillet with sauce; add 1/3 cup Parmesan cheese. Toss noodles, sauce and cheese over medium heat until sauce coats noodles, 20 to 30 seconds. Serve immediately with additional Parmesan cheese. Makes 8 servings.

How to Make Green Tagliatelle with Salmon Sauce

1/Put pasta sheets through widest cutting blade of pasta machine.

2/Arrange noodles in soft bundles to dry.

Tagliatelle Bologna-Style

Tagliatelle alla Bolognese

For a family meal follow this satisfying dish with some cheese and a green salad.

Basic Egg Pasta Dough, page 30, made with 3 cups all-purpose flour
2 cups Bolognese Meat Sauce, page 160

1/3 cup freshly grated Parmesan cheese
Additional Parmesan cheese

Prepare noodles, page 29, from Basic Egg Pasta Dough, page 30. Prepare Bolognese Meat Sauce and keep warm. Fill a very large saucepan two-thirds full with salted water. Bring water to a boil. Add noodles. Bring water back to a boil and cook noodles uncovered until tender but firm to the bite, page 29. Drain noodles and place in a warm deep dish or bowl. Add sauce and 1/3 cup Parmesan cheese. Toss gently until mixed. Serve immediately with additional Parmesan cheese. Makes 6 servings.

Tagliatelle with Scallops & Cream Sauce

Tagliatelle con Cape Sante alla Crema

An elegant dish that should be served for special people and for special occasions.

Basic Egg Pasta Dough, page 30,
   made with 3 cups all-purpose flour
1 lb. scallops
1/4 cup butter

3 garlic cloves, finely chopped
1 cup whipping cream
3 tablespoons chopped parsley
Salt and white pepper to taste

Prepare noodles, page 29, from Basic Egg Pasta Dough, page 30. Wash scallops in cold water and dry well. Slice scallops into thirds if small, or fourths if large. Melt butter in a large skillet. When butter foams, add sliced scallops and garlic. Cook 2 minutes over medium heat until lightly colored, stirring occasionally. Stir in cream, parsley and salt and white pepper. Cook 1 minute longer or until cream begins to thicken. Fill a very large saucepan two-thirds full with salted water. Bring water to a boil. Add noodles. Bring water back to a boil and cook noodles uncovered until tender but firm to the bite, page 29. Drain noodles and place in skillet with sauce. Toss noodles and sauce over medium heat until sauce coats noodles, 20 to 30 seconds. Serve immediately. Makes 6 servings.

Green Tagliatelle with Tomato Sauce

Tagliatelle Verdi con Salsa Burro e Oro

Photo on pages 180 and 181.

Follow this surprisingly delicate dish with any roast meat or poultry.

Basic Spinach Pasta Dough, page 30,
   made with 2 cups all-purpose flour
1-1/2 cups Plain Tomato Sauce, page 161
1/4 cup butter

1/2 cup whipping cream
Salt and freshly ground pepper to taste
1/3 cup freshly grated Parmesan cheese
Additional Parmesan cheese

Prepare noodles, page 29, from Basic Spinach Pasta Dough, page 30. Prepare Plain Tomato Sauce. Melt butter in a medium saucepan. When butter foams, add tomato sauce and cream. Season with salt and pepper. Simmer uncovered 8 to 10 minutes. Fill a very large saucepan two-thirds full with salted water. Bring water to a boil. Add noodles. Bring water back to a boil and cook noodles uncovered until tender but firm to the bite, page 29. Drain noodles and place in a warm deep dish or bowl. Add sauce and toss gently until mixed. Add 1/3 cup Parmesan cheese and toss to blend. Serve immediately with additional Parmesan cheese. Makes 4 servings.

When a sauce is too thin, thicken it by boiling it uncovered until it reaches the desired consistency. This will also intensify the flavor.

Pappardelle with Tomatoes & Basil

Pappardelle al Pomodoro e Basilico

Prepare this for a dish alive with taste and color.

Fresh Tomato Sauce, see below
Basic Egg Pasta Dough, page 30, made with
   3 cups all-purpose flour

Fresh Tomato Sauce:
1-1/2 lbs. tomatoes
2 garlic cloves, finely chopped
6 large black olives
1/3 cup loosely packed fresh basil or
   2 tablespoons finely chopped parsley

1/3 cup olive oil
Salt and freshly ground pepper to taste

Prepare Fresh Tomato Sauce and let stand at room temperature. Prepare noodles, page 29, from Basic Egg Pasta Dough, page 30. Fill a very large saucepan two-thirds full with salted water. Bring water to a boil. Add noodles. Bring water back to a boil and cook noodles uncovered until tender but firm to the bite, page 29. Drain noodles and place in a warm deep dish or bowl. Add tomato sauce and toss gently until mixed. Serve immediately. Makes 4 to 6 servings.

Fresh Tomato Sauce:
Peel, seed and dice tomatoes, as for Penne with Hot Pepper & Tomatoes, page 42. Place tomatoes in a medium bowl. Add garlic, olives, basil or parsley and oil. Season with salt and pepper. Stir well.

Pappardelle with Mushroom Sauce

Pappardelle con i Funghi

Pappardelle are the widest of all noodles.

Basic Egg Pasta Dough, page 30, made with
   3 cups all-purpose flour
1-1/2 lbs. small white mushrooms
5 tablespoons olive oil
2 garlic cloves, finely chopped

3/4 cup dry white wine
3 tablespoons chopped parsley
Salt and freshly ground pepper to taste
2 tablespoons butter

Prepare Basic Egg Pasta Dough. Dry pasta sheets 10 minutes. With a fluted pastry wheel, cut each sheet of pasta into broad strips 1/2 inch wide to make pappardelle. Arrange noodles in soft piles on a large tablecloth. Wash and dry mushrooms thoroughly and slice thin. Heat oil in a large skillet. Add garlic and sauté over medium heat about 1 minute. When garlic begins to color, add sliced mushrooms. Sauté mushrooms over high heat until lightly colored. Add wine. Cook until wine is reduced by half, stirring constantly. Add parsley and cook 1 minute longer. Season with salt and pepper. Fill a very large saucepan two-thirds full with salted water. Bring water to a boil. Add noodles. Bring water back to a boil and cook noodles uncovered until tender but firm to the bite, page 29. Drain noodles and place in skillet with sauce; add butter. Toss noodles, sauce and butter over medium heat until sauce coats noodles, 20 to 30 seconds. Serve immediately. Makes 6 servings.

Macaroni Pie

Pasticcio di Maccheroni

Bologna is renowned for its spectacular pork dishes. Here is a great example.

Pie Pastry, see below
2 tablespoons butter
1/2 lb. pork loin, finely chopped
1 medium onion, finely chopped
1/2 cup dry white wine
1 cup canned crushed Italian-style or
    whole tomatoes, drained
1/2 lb. small white mushrooms
2 tablespoons butter

2 tablespoons chopped parsley
Salt and freshly ground pepper to taste
3 quarts milk
2 tablespoons salt
1 lb. macaroni, such as penne
Basic White Sauce, page 158, made with
    3 cups milk
1 egg, lightly beaten

Pie Pastry:
2 cups all-purpose flour
2/3 cup butter, room temperature for
    hand mixing, cold and
    in small pieces for food processor

1 egg
1/2 teaspoon salt
3 to 4 tablespoons chilled white wine

Prepare Pie Pastry. Melt 2 tablespoons butter in a small skillet. When butter foams, add pork and onion. Cook and stir over medium heat until meat is no longer pink. Increase heat and add wine. When wine is reduced by half, cover skillet and reduce heat. Cook 10 minutes. Press tomatoes through a food mill or sieve, page 161, to remove seeds. Wash and dry mushrooms thoroughly and cut into wedges. Melt 2 tablespoons butter in a large skillet. Add mushrooms. Sautè over high heat 2 to 3 minutes or until golden. Reduce heat. Add parsley, pork mixture and tomato pulp. Season with salt and pepper. Simmer 5 to 10 minutes. Bring milk to a boil in a very large saucepan. Add 2 tablespoons salt and macaroni. Bring milk back to a boil and cook macaroni uncovered until quite firm to the bite, 5 to 6 minutes. Drain macaroni, reserving milk, and place in skillet with pork mixture. Toss gently until mixed; set aside. Prepare Basic White Sauce using milk in which macaroni was cooked. Stir white sauce into macaroni mixture. Preheat oven to 375F (190C). Butter a 10-inch cake pan with a removable bottom. On a lightly floured surface, roll out larger amount of pastry dough into a 14-inch circle. Place dough carefully in buttered pan. Pour macaroni mixture into pastry shell and level top with a spatula. Roll out remaining pastry dough to a 10-1/2-inch circle and place on top of macaroni mixture. Pinch edges of bottom and top dough together to seal. Brush dough with beaten egg. With a fork, puncture top crust of pie in 5 or 6 places. Bake 40 to 50 minutes or until crust is golden. Let stand 5 to 10 minutes in pan. Remove pie from pan and place on a large round platter. Cut into wedges and serve. Makes 6 servings.

Pie Pastry:
In a medium bowl using a pastry blender or in a food processor fitted with a metal blade, mix flour and butter until crumbly. Add egg, salt and wine; mix until dough is completely moistened. Place dough on a flat surface and work into 2 balls, one a little larger than the other. Wrap in waxed paper and refrigerate at least 1 hour.

Baked Macaroni

Maccheroni al Forno

Try to resist a second helping!

2 cups Chicken Broth, page 20, or
   canned chicken broth
1/4 cup butter
1 medium onion, finely chopped
1 carrot, finely chopped
1/4 lb. pancetta, page 6,
   cut into 4 slices and diced

1/4 cup tomato paste
Salt and freshly ground pepper to taste
1 lb. large, grooved macaroni
Basic White Sauce, page 158, made with
   2 cups milk
1/2 cup freshly grated Parmesan cheese
2 tablespoons butter

Prepare Chicken Broth. Preheat oven to 375F (190C). Butter a 13" x 9" baking dish. Melt 1/4 cup butter in a medium saucepan. When butter foams, add onion and carrot. Sauté over medium heat until onion is pale yellow. Add pancetta. Sauté until lightly colored. Combine tomato paste and broth and add to saucepan. Simmer uncovered 20 to 25 minutes. Season with salt and pepper. Fill a very large saucepan two-thirds full with salted water. Bring water to a boil. Add macaroni. Bring water back to a boil and cook macaroni uncovered until tender but firm to the bite, 6 to 8 minutes. Drain macaroni and place in buttered baking dish. Prepare Basic White Sauce. Stir tomato sauce and white sauce into macaroni; mix to blend. Add 1/3 cup Parmesan cheese; mix gently. Sprinkle remaining Parmesan cheese over macaroni and dot with 2 tablespoons butter. Bake 10 to 15 minutes or until cheese is melted and top is golden. Serve hot. Makes 4 servings.

Macaroni with Vodka Sauce

Maccheroni con la Vodka

This simple sauce is a creation of the Dante restaurant in Bologna.

1-1/2 cups Plain Tomato Sauce, page 161
1/4 cup butter
1/4 lb. pancetta, page 6,
   cut into 4 slices and diced
1/3 cup vodka

1/2 cup whipping cream
Salt and freshly ground pepper to taste
1 lb. grooved macaroni, such as
   penne or rigatoni
1/2 cup freshly grated Parmesan cheese

Prepare Plain Tomato Sauce. Melt butter in a large skillet. When butter foams, add pancetta. Sauté over medium heat until lightly colored. Add vodka and stir until it has evaporated. Stir in tomato sauce and cream. Simmer uncovered 8 to 10 minutes. Season with salt and pepper. Fill a very large saucepan two-thirds full with salted water. Bring water to a boil. Add macaroni. Bring water back to a boil and cook macaroni uncovered until tender but firm to the bite, 8 to 10 minutes. Drain macaroni and place in skillet with sauce. Toss macaroni and sauce over medium heat until sauce coats macaroni, 20 to 30 seconds. Serve immediately with Parmesan cheese. Makes 4 to 6 servings.

Macaroni with Ham & Asparagus

Maccheroni con Prosciutto Cotto e Asparagi

It takes longer to prepare a frozen dinner than to cook this absolutely delectable dish.

1-1/2 lbs. small asparagus
1/4 cup butter
2 medium onions, thinly sliced
1/2 lb. boiled ham, diced
1 cup whipping cream

Salt and freshly ground pepper to taste
1 lb. medium-size macaroni, such as penne
1/3 cup freshly grated Parmesan cheese
Additional Parmesan cheese

Wash asparagus and cut tips off stalks. Reserve stalks for another use. Fill a medium saucepan half full with salted water. Bring water to a boil. Add asparagus tips. Boil about 1 minute or until tender but firm. Drain asparagus. Melt butter in a large skillet. When butter foams, add onions. Sauté over medium heat until pale yellow. Add drained asparagus and ham. Sauté 1 to 2 minutes. Stir in cream. Simmer 2 minutes or until cream begins to thicken. Season with salt and pepper. Fill a very large saucepan two-thirds full with salted water. Bring water to a boil. Add macaroni. Bring water back to a boil and cook macaroni uncovered until tender but firm to the bite, 8 to 10 minutes. Drain macaroni and place in skillet with sauce. Add 1/3 cup Parmesan cheese. Toss macaroni and sauce over medium heat until sauce coats macaroni, 20 to 30 seconds. Serve immediately with additional Parmesan cheese. Makes 4 to 6 servings.

Tagliarini with Tomato, Cream & Peas

Tagliarini al Burro e Oro e Piselli

Tagliarini are thin noodles generally served in broth.

1-1/2 cups Plain Tomato Sauce, page 161
Basic Egg Pasta Dough, page 30, made with
   2-1/4 cups all-purpose flour
3 tablespoons butter
1/2 cup whipping cream

1 cup small frozen peas, thawed
Salt and freshly ground pepper to taste
1/3 cup freshly grated Parmesan cheese
Additional Parmesan cheese

Prepare Plain Tomato Sauce. Prepare Basic Egg Pasta Dough. Dry pasta sheets 10 to 15 minutes. Feed pasta sheets through the narrow cutting blades of the pasta machine to make tagliarini. Arrange noodles in soft piles on a large tablecloth. Melt butter in a large skillet. When butter foams, add tomato sauce, cream and peas. Mix to blend. Season with salt and pepper. Simmer 4 to 5 minutes or until sauce reduces to a medium-thick consistency. Fill a very large saucepan two-thirds full with salted water. Bring water to a boil. Add noodles. Bring water back to a boil and cook noodles uncovered until tender but firm to the bite, page 29. Drain noodles and place in skillet with sauce; add 1/3 cup Parmesan cheese. Toss noodles, sauce and cheese over medium heat until sauce coats noodles, 20 to 30 seconds. Serve immediately with additional Parmesan cheese. Makes 4 servings.

Strichetti with Garlic & Tomato Sauce

Strichetti all'Aglio e Pomodoro

When I first learned to make pasta, this was my favorite one to make and eat.

Basic Egg Pasta Dough, page 30, made with
   3 cups all-purpose flour
2 cups Tomato Sauce Bologna-Style, page 157
1/3 cup olive oil

6 garlic cloves, finely chopped
2 tablespoons chopped parsley
Salt and freshly ground pepper to taste
1/2 cup freshly grated Parmesan cheese

Prepare Basic Egg Pasta Dough. Cut a small piece of dough and work through the pasta machine until you have a thin sheet of pasta. Cut pasta sheet into rectangles 2 inches wide and 2-1/2 inches long. Pinch the 2 long sides of each rectangle together in the center making butterfly shapes or strichetti. Repeat with remaining dough, rolling out and shaping 1 sheet of pasta at a time. Spread strichetti in a single layer on a large tablecloth to dry. Prepare Tomato Sauce Bologna-Style. Heat oil in a medium saucepan. Add garlic and parsley. Sauté 1 minute over medium heat. Just before garlic changes color, add tomato sauce and salt and pepper. Cook uncovered 5 to 8 minutes. Fill a very large saucepan two-thirds full with salted water. Bring water to a boil. Add strichetti. Bring water back to a boil and cook strichetti uncovered until tender but firm to the bite, page 29. Drain strichetti and place in a warm deep dish or bowl. Add sauce. Toss strichetti and sauce gently until mixed. Serve immediately with Parmesan cheese. Makes 6 servings.

Penne with Hot Pepper & Tomatoes

Penne all'Arrabbiata

Penne are macaroni shaped like quills that come ridged or smooth.

1-1/2 lbs. tomatoes
1/3 cup olive oil
1/2 small red or green hot pepper, chopped
2 garlic cloves, finely chopped

Salt to taste
2 tablespoons chopped parsley
1 lb. penne

Cut out tomato cores with a sharp knife. Fill a large saucepan two-thirds full with water. Bring water to a boil. Add tomatoes. Boil 20 to 25 seconds or until skins begin to split. Place tomatoes in a bowl of cold water. Peel cooled tomatoes and cut in half horizontally. Squeeze seeds and juice out of each tomato half. Dice tomatoes. Heat oil in a large skillet. Add hot pepper and garlic. Sauté over medium heat about 1 minute. Before garlic changes color, add diced tomatoes. Season with salt. Cook uncovered over medium heat 8 to 10 minutes. Stir in parsley and cook 1 to 2 minutes longer. Fill a very large saucepan two-thirds full with salted water. Bring water to a boil. Add penne. Bring water back to a boil and cook penne uncovered until tender but firm to the bite, 8 to 10 minutes. Drain penne and place in skillet with sauce. Toss penne and sauce over medium heat until sauce coats penne, 20 to 30 seconds. Serve immediately. Makes 4 to 6 servings.

How to Make Strichetti with Garlic & Tomato Sauce

1/Cut pasta sheets into rectangles.

2/Pinch long sides of pasta rectangles together to make butterfly shapes.

Rigatoni with Peperonata

Rigatoni con la Peperonata

Peperonata is too good to use only as a side dish so here it is transformed into a superb pasta dish.

2 cups Peperonata, page 127
1 lb. rigatoni or any large,
  grooved macaroni

Freshly ground pepper to taste

Prepare Peperonata and keep warm. Fill a very large saucepan two-thirds full with salted water. Bring water to a boil. Add rigatoni. Bring water back to a boil and cook rigatoni uncovered until tender but firm to the bite, 8 to 10 minutes. Drain rigatoni and place in a warm deep dish or bowl. Pour Peperonata over rigatoni. Season with pepper. Serve immediately. Makes 4 to 6 servings.

Photographed on the following pages, clockwise starting at the top, Spaghetti with Spring Vegetables, page 48; Green Lasagne Bologna-Style, page 49; and Agnolotti Genoa-Style, page 54.

Fettuccine with Butter & Cream

Fettuccine all'Alfredo

Fettuccine is the Roman name for noodles.

**Basic Egg Pasta Dough, page 30, made with
  2-1/4 cups all-purpose flour
1/4 cup butter
1 cup whipping cream**

**Salt and white pepper to taste
1/4 cup freshly grated Parmesan cheese
Additional Parmesan cheese**

Prepare noodles, page 29, from Basic Egg Pasta Dough, page 30. Melt butter in a large skillet. When butter foams, add cream. Simmer over medium heat about 2 minutes until slightly thickened. Season with salt and white pepper. Fill a very large saucepan two-thirds full with salted water. Bring water to a boil. Add noodles. Bring water back to a boil and cook noodles uncovered until tender but firm to the bite, page 29. Drain noodles and place in skillet with cream. Add 1/4 cup Parmesan cheese. Toss noodles and sauce over medium heat until sauce coats noodles, 20 to 30 seconds. Serve immediately with additional Parmesan cheese. Makes 4 to 6 servings.

Green Fettuccine with Red Clam Sauce

Fettuccine Verdi alla Marinara

If fresh basil is not available, double the amount of parsley.

**Basic Spinach Pasta Dough, page 30,
  made with 2 cups all-purpose flour
4 lbs. small fresh clams
1 cup dry white wine
6 tablespoons olive oil**

**3 tablespoons chopped fresh basil
2 tablespoons chopped parsley
2 garlic cloves, finely chopped
2 tablespoons tomato paste
Salt and freshly ground pepper to taste**

Prepare noodles, page 29, from Basic Spinach Pasta Dough, page 30. Soak clams in cold water 15 minutes. Scrub clams with a brush and rinse thoroughly. Put clams, wine and 2 tablespoons oil in a large saucepan. Cover pan. Cook over high heat until clams open, 1 or 2 minutes. Remove clam meat from shells. Strain pan juices and reserve. Heat 1/4 cup oil in a medium saucepan. Add basil, parsley and garlic. Sauté over medium heat about 1 minute. Add reserved clam juice, tomato paste and salt and pepper. Stir to blend. Cook uncovered 8 to 10 minutes. Add clam meat and cook 1 minute longer. Fill a very large saucepan two-thirds full with salted water. Bring water to a boil. Add noodles. Bring water back to a boil and cook noodles uncovered until tender but firm to the bite, page 29. Drain noodles and place in a warm deep dish or bowl. Add sauce and toss gently until mixed. Serve immediately. Makes 4 servings.

Baked Cannelloni

Cannelloni al Forno

An elegant party dish that can be prepared ahead.

2 cups Plain Tomato Sauce, page 161
Basic White Sauce, page 158, made with
  3 cups milk
Meat Filling, see below

Basic Egg Pasta Dough, page 30, made
  with 4-1/2 cups all-purpose flour
1/2 cup freshly grated Parmesan cheese
3 tablespoons butter

Meat Filling:

3 tablespoons butter
1 lb. chicken breasts, boned, skinned,
  chopped into small pieces
1/4 lb. prosciutto, page 6, diced
1/4 lb. mortadella, diced

1/2 cup freshly grated Parmesan cheese
1/2 teaspoon freshly grated nutmeg
2 or 3 tablespoons whipping cream,
  if needed
Salt and freshly ground pepper to taste

Prepare Plain Tomato Sauce. Prepare Basic White Sauce. Prepare Meat Filling. Prepare Basic Egg Pasta Dough. Dry pasta sheets 10 minutes. Cut sheets into 5" x 5" squares. Preheat oven to 400F (205C). Butter a 13" x 9" baking dish. Fill a very large saucepan two-thirds full with salted water. Bring water to a boil. Add 7 or 8 pasta squares. Bring water back to a boil and cook pasta uncovered 10 seconds. With a large slotted spoon, place pasta in a large bowl of cold water. Remove pasta squares immediately and lay on kitchen towels. Pat dry with another towel. Repeat with remaining pasta squares. Place 1 or 2 tablespoons Meat Filling down center of each dried pasta square. Fold 2 opposite edges of pasta over filling to make a tube. Place cannelloni with folded edges down, close together in a single layer in buttered baking dish. Spoon tomato sauce over cannelloni. Cover with white sauce. Sprinkle with Parmesan cheese and dot with butter. Bake 10 to 15 minutes or until cheese is melted and cannelloni are lightly golden. Let stand 5 to 10 minutes before serving. Makes about 20 cannelloni, 6 to 8 servings.

Meat Filling:

Melt butter in a medium skillet. When butter foams, add chicken pieces. Sauté over medium heat until lightly colored. Put chicken and all other ingredients except cream in a blender or food processor. Blend to a paste. If mixture is too dry, add cream. Season with salt and pepper.

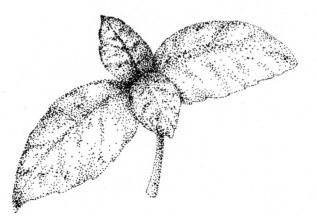

Spaghetti with Spring Vegetables   Photo on pages 44 and 45.

Spaghetti Primavera

This dish captures the bountifulness of spring.

5 medium tomatoes
1/4 lb. small asparagus
1 medium zucchini
1/4 lb. small white mushrooms
1 large red or green sweet pepper
5 tablespoons olive oil

1 medium onion, thinly sliced
Salt and freshly ground pepper to taste
3 tablespoons chopped parsley
2 garlic cloves, finely chopped
1 lb. spaghetti

Peel, seed and dice tomatoes, page 42. Wash asparagus and cut tips off stalks. Reserve stalks for another use. Wash and dry zucchini and mushrooms thoroughly; cut into thin slices. Wash pepper and cut into short thin strips. Heat oil in large skillet. Add pepper strips and sauté over medium heat 5 to 6 minutes. Add onion, zucchini, asparagus tips and mushrooms. Sauté 4 to 5 minutes. Add diced tomatoes and salt and pepper. Cook uncovered over medium heat 10 minutes, stirring frequently. Stir in parsley and garlic. Taste and adjust for seasoning. Fill a very large saucepan two-thirds full with salted water. Bring water to a boil. Add spaghetti. Bring water back to a boil and cook spaghetti uncovered until tender but firm to the bite, 8 to 10 minutes. Drain spaghetti and place in a warm deep dish or bowl. Pour sauce over spaghetti. Serve immediately. Makes 4 to 6 servings.

Spaghetti with Tuna Fish Sauce

Spaghetti con il Tonno

Do not serve cheese over this pasta; be generous with the pepper instead.

1/4 cup olive oil
4 flat anchovy fillets, finely chopped
2 garlic cloves, finely chopped
1 (28-oz.) can crushed Italian-style or
   whole tomatoes

Salt and freshly ground pepper to taste
1 (7-oz.) can tuna fish in olive oil,
   drained, flaked
3 tablespoons chopped parsley
1 lb. spaghetti

Heat oil in a medium saucepan. Add anchovies and garlic. Sauté gently about 1 minute; do not let garlic turn brown. Press tomatoes through a food mill or sieve, page 161, to remove seeds. Stir tomato pulp into saucepan. Simmer uncovered 25 to 30 minutes or until sauce reduces to a medium-thick consistency. Season with salt and pepper. Stir in tuna fish and parsley. Simmer 5 minutes. Fill a very large saucepan two-thirds full with salted water. Bring water to a boil. Add spaghetti. Bring water back to a boil and cook spaghetti uncovered until tender but firm to the bite, 8 to 10 minutes. Drain spaghetti and place in a warm deep dish or bowl. Add sauce and toss gently until mixed. Serve immediately. Makes 4 servings.

Spaghetti with Bacon & Egg Sauce

Spaghetti alla Carbonara

I have never found two chefs who serve the same version of this popular Roman dish.

2 tablespoons butter
1 tablespoon olive oil
1/2 lb. pancetta, page 6, cut into
  4 or 5 slices and diced
4 egg yolks

1/3 cup whipping cream
1/3 cup freshly grated Parmesan cheese
Salt and freshly ground pepper to taste
1 lb. spaghetti
Additional Parmesan cheese

Melt butter with oil in a small saucepan. When butter foams, add pancetta. Sauté over medium heat until lightly colored. Keep warm. Beat egg yolks in a large shallow serving dish. Beat in cream, 1/3 cup Parmesan cheese and salt and pepper. This dish should be quite peppery. Fill a very large saucepan two-thirds full with salted water. Bring water to a boil. Add spaghetti. Bring water back to a boil and cook spaghetti uncovered until tender but firm to the bite, 8 to 10 minutes. Drain spaghetti and place in dish with egg yolk mixture. Toss quickly. Add sautéed pancetta and toss gently until mixed. Serve immediately with additional Parmesan cheese. Makes 4 to 6 servings.

Green Lasagne Bologna-Style Photo on pages 44 and 45.

Lasagne Verdi alla Bolognese

In this celebrated dish, each ingredient complements the other without losing its individuality.

4 to 4-1/2 cups Bolognese Meat Sauce,
  page 160
Basic White Sauce, page 158, made with
  5 cups milk

Basic Spinach Pasta Dough, page 30,
  made with 3 cups all-purpose flour
2 cups freshly grated Parmesan cheese
3 tablespoons butter

Prepare Bolognese Meat Sauce. Prepare Basic White Sauce. Prepare Basic Spinach Pasta Dough and cut into lengths to fit a 13" x 9" baking dish. Dry pasta sheets 10 minutes. Preheat oven to 400F (205C). Butter baking dish. Fill a very large saucepan two-thirds full with salted water. Bring water to a boil. Add 4 pasta sheets. Bring water back to a boil and cook pasta uncovered 10 seconds. With a large slotted spoon, place pasta in a large bowl of cold water. Remove pasta sheets immediately and lay on kitchen towels. Pat dry with another towel. Repeat with remaining pasta sheets. Cover bottom of buttered baking dish with a layer of dried pasta sheets. Spread some meat sauce over pasta. Follow with a layer of Basic White Sauce, about 1/2 cup. Sprinkle with about 1/3 cup Parmesan cheese. Repeat with 5 more layers, ending with Parmesan cheese. Dot with butter. Bake 15 to 20 minutes or until top of lasagne is golden. Let stand 5 to 10 minutes before serving. Makes 8 servings.

Tortellini with Cream Sauce

Tortellini alla Panna

Tortellini are instantly recognized as the best contribution of Bolognese cuisine to Italian gastronomy.

Meat Filling, see below
Basic Egg Pasta Dough, page 30, made with
   3 cups all-purpose flour

Cream Sauce, see below
1/3 cup freshly grated Parmesan cheese
Additional Parmesan cheese

Meat Filling:
2 tablespoons butter
1 lb. pork loin, finely chopped
1/2 cup dry white wine
2 eggs
1/2 teaspoon freshly grated nutmeg

1/4 lb. mortadella
1/4 lb. prosciutto, page 6
3/4 cup freshly grated Parmesan cheese
2 to 3 tablespoons whipping cream, if needed
Salt and freshly ground pepper to taste

Cream Sauce:
1/4 cup butter
1 cup whipping cream

1 teaspoon salt

Prepare Meat Filling and refrigerate. Prepare Basic Egg Pasta Dough. Cut a small piece of dough and work through the pasta machine until you have a very thin sheet of pasta. Cut pasta into 2-inch circles using a small glass or cookie cutter. Put 1/2 teaspoon filling in the center of each circle. Fold circles in half and press firmly to seal edges to make tortellini. Bend each tortellini around your finger, pressing 1 pointed end over the other. Repeat with remaining dough, rolling out and filling 1 sheet of pasta at a time. Dust 2 or 3 large plates or trays with flour. Place tortellini on plates or trays. Turn tortellini over every couple of hours, until completely dry. Refrigerate uncovered until ready to use. Prepare Cream Sauce. Fill a very large saucepan two-thirds full with salted water. Bring water to a boil. Add tortellini. Bring water back to a boil and cook tortellini uncovered until tender but firm to the bite, page 29. Drain tortellini and place in skillet with sauce. Add 1/3 cup Parmesan cheese. Toss tortellini and sauce over low heat until sauce coats tortellini, 20 to 30 seconds. Serve immediately with additional Parmesan cheese. Makes 5 to 6 servings.

Meat Filling:
Melt butter in a small skillet. When butter foams, add pork. Sauté over medium heat until light golden. Add wine. Reduce heat and cook covered 10 to 12 minutes. Put pork mixture and all other ingredients except cream in a blender or food processor. Blend to a paste. If mixture is too dry, add cream. Season with salt and pepper.

Cream Sauce:
Melt butter in a large skillet. When butter foams, add cream. Simmer 2 or 3 minutes until slightly thickened. Add salt.

How to Make Tortellini with Cream Sauce

1/Fold pasta circles in half over filling and press firmly to seal.

2/Bend tortellini around your finger, pressing pointed ends over each other.

Tortellini with Bolognese Meat Sauce

Tortellini col Ragù

With a few advance preparations you can relax and enjoy your company.

Tortellini, page 50
1-1/2 to 2 cups Bolognese Meat Sauce,
   page 160

1/2 cup freshly grated Parmesan cheese

Prepare and fill tortellini. Prepare Bolognese Meat Sauce and keep warm. Fill a very large saucepan two-thirds full with salted water. Bring water to a boil. Add tortellini. Bring water back to a boil and cook tortellini uncovered until tender but firm to the bite, page 29. Drain tortellini and place in a warm deep dish or bowl. Add meat sauce and toss gently until mixed. Serve immediately with Parmesan cheese. Makes 5 to 6 servings.

Tortelloni with Ricotta Cheese & Parsley Photo on cover.

Tortelloni di Ricotta e Prezzemolo

Tortelloni are traditionally served in Bologna on the night before Christmas.

Cheese Filling, see below
2 cups Tomato-Cream Sauce, see below
Basic Egg Pasta Dough, page 30, made with
   3 cups all-purpose flour

2 tablespoons butter
1/3 cup freshly grated Parmesan cheese
Additional Parmesan cheese

Cheese Filling:
1 egg yolk
1 lb. ricotta cheese
1/3 cup chopped parsley

1/2 cup freshly grated Parmesan cheese
1/2 teaspoon freshly grated nutmeg
Salt to taste

Tomato-Cream Sauce:
2 tablespoons butter
1-1/2 cups Plain Tomato Sauce, page 161

1/2 cup whipping cream
Salt and freshly ground pepper to taste

Prepare Cheese Filling and refrigerate. Prepare Tomato-Cream Sauce and let stand at room temperature. Prepare Basic Egg Pasta Dough. Cut a small piece of dough and work through the pasta machine until you have a very thin sheet of pasta. Cut pasta into 3-inch circles using a glass or a cookie cutter. Put 1 teaspoon filling in the center of each circle. Fold circles in half and press firmly to seal edges to make tortelloni. Bend each tortelloni around your finger, pressing 1 pointed end over the other. Repeat with remaining dough, rolling out and filling 1 sheet of pasta at a time. Dust 2 or 3 large plates or trays with flour. Place tortelloni on plates or trays. Turn tortelloni over every couple of hours until completely dry. Refrigerate uncovered until ready to use. Fill a very large saucepan two-thirds full with salted water. Bring water to a boil. Add tortelloni. Bring water back to a boil and cook tortelloni uncovered until tender but firm to the bite, page 29. Drain tortelloni and place in a warm deep dish or bowl. Add butter, Tomato-Cream Sauce and 1/3 cup Parmesan cheese. Toss gently until mixed. Serve immediately with additional Parmesan cheese. Makes 6 servings.

Cheese Filling:
Beat egg yolk in a large bowl. Add ricotta cheese, parsley, Parmesan cheese and nutmeg; mix to blend. Season with salt.

Tomato-Cream Sauce:
Melt butter in a medium saucepan. Add Plain Tomato Sauce and cream. Season with salt and pepper. Simmer 5 to 10 minutes.

Variation
Make green tortelloni using Basic Spinach Pasta Dough, page 30, made with 3 cups all-purpose flour.

Linguine with Red Clam Sauce

Linguine con le Vongole

Linguine belong to the same family as spaghetti but are flat.

1 cup Plain Tomato Sauce, page 161
4 lbs. small fresh clams
2 tablespoons olive oil
1 cup water
3 tablespoons olive oil

3 garlic cloves, finely chopped
2 tablespoons chopped parsley
3 flat anchovy fillets, finely chopped
Salt and freshly ground pepper to taste
1 lb. linguine

Prepare Plain Tomato Sauce. Soak clams in cold water 15 minutes. Scrub clams with a brush and rinse thoroughly. Put clams, 2 tablespoons oil and 1 cup water in a large saucepan; cover pan. Cook over high heat until clams open, 1 to 2 minutes. Remove clam meat from shells. Strain pan juices and place in a small saucepan. Bring to a boil and cook uncovered until liquid is reduced to about 1/2 cup. Set aside. Heat 3 tablespoons oil in a medium saucepan. Add garlic, parsley and anchovies. Sauté over medium heat about 1 minute. When garlic changes color, add tomato sauce, reserved clam juice and salt and pepper. Cook 5 minutes. Add clam meat and cook 1 to 2 minutes longer. Fill a very large saucepan two-thirds full with salted water. Bring water to a boil. Add linguine. Bring water back to a boil and cook linguine uncovered until tender but firm to the bite, 8 to 10 minutes. Drain linguine and place in a warm deep dish or bowl. Add sauce and toss gently until mixed. Serve immediately. Makes 4 to 6 servings.

Agnolotti Genoa-Style   Photo on pages 44 and 45.

Agnolotti alla Genovese

In many regions, agnolotti and ravioli are the same shape but their fillings are different.

Meat Filling, see below
Basic Egg Pasta Dough, page 30, made with
   3 cups all-purpose flour

1/4 cup butter, room temperature
1/2 cup freshly grated Parmesan cheese
Additional Parmesan cheese

Meat Filling:
1/2 cup Chicken Broth, page 20, or
   canned chicken broth
1 (10-oz.) pkg. frozen spinach, thawed
3 tablespoons butter
2 large onions, thinly sliced
1 lb. pork loin, cut in 1-inch cubes
3/4 cup dry white wine

1 tablespoon chopped parsley
2 tablespoons chopped fresh basil or parsley
2 eggs
1/2 teaspoon dried chervil
Salt and freshly ground pepper to taste
3/4 cup freshly grated Parmesan cheese

Prepare Meat Filling and refrigerate. Prepare Basic Egg Pasta Dough. Cut small pieces of dough and work through the pasta machine until you have thin sheets of pasta. Cut pasta sheets into strips 4 inches wide. Place 1 teaspoon filling every 2 inches down the center of each strip of pasta. Fold sheets in half over filling. Press edges together to seal. With a pastry cutter, cut pasta strips into squares, cutting between filling to make agnolotti. Dust 2 or 3 large plates or trays with flour. Place agnolotti on plates or trays. Turn agnolotti over every 2 to 3 hours until completely dry. Refrigerate uncovered until ready to use. Fill a very large saucepan two-thirds full with salted water. Bring water to a boil. Add agnolotti. Bring water back to a boil and cook agnolotti uncovered until tender but firm to the bite, page 29. Drain agnolotti and place in a warm deep dish or bowl. Add butter and 1/2 cup Parmesan cheese. Toss gently until mixed. Serve immediately with additional Parmesan cheese. Makes 6 servings.

Meat Filling:
Prepare Chicken Broth. Squeeze spinach to remove as much moisture as possible. Melt butter in a medium skillet. When butter foams, add onions and pork. Sauté 3 to 4 minutes over medium heat until light golden. Stir in wine. Cook until wine has evaporated. Add broth. Cook uncovered 15 minutes or until all moisture has evaporated. Stir occasionally. Add spinach, parsley and basil or extra parsley. Cook 1 to 2 minutes longer. Put pork mixture in a blender or food processor. Add eggs and chervil and blend to a paste. Season with salt and pepper. Place mixture in a bowl. Add Parmesan cheese and mix thoroughly.

Pasta stuffed with spinach and cheese should not be prepared more than one day ahead. Refrigerate covered with a kitchen towel.

How to Make Agnolotti Genoa-Style

1/Place teaspoonfuls of filling along pasta strip.

2/Cut pasta between filling to make agnolotti.

Trenette with Pesto Sauce

Trenette col Pesto

If you lived in the Liguria region of Italy you would call noodles trenette.

Basic Egg Pasta Dough, page 30, made with 3 cups all-purpose flour   **1/2 to 3/4 cup Pesto Sauce, page 159**

Prepare noodles, page 29, from Basic Egg Pasta Dough, page 30. Prepare Pesto Sauce and let stand at room temperature. Fill a very large saucepan two-thirds full with salted water. Bring water to a boil. Add noodles. Bring water back to a boil and cook noodles uncovered until tender but firm to the bite, page 29. Drain noodles and place in a warm deep dish or bowl. Add Pesto Sauce and toss gently until mixed. Serve immediately. Makes 6 servings.

Gnocchi

Gnocchi is the general name for Italian dumplings. There are many kinds including potato, spinach and spinach with cheese. This light Italian version of dumplings is a melt-in-your-mouth delicacy. Gnocchi are served as a first course with an incredible array of sauces. In a way, gnocchi and pasta are very much alike. They could be eaten with a different sauce every day for weeks without a dish being repeated. When you serve gnocchi, follow the same guidelines as for serving pasta. Gnocchi are only the first course so serve moderate portions with a small amount of sauce.

With practice, you will find gnocchi are really simple to make. Have fun experimenting with the recipes in this chapter. Then go on to dazzle family and friends with superb dishes.

Polenta

Polenta is made from cornmeal and probably dates back further than any dish in Italian cuisine. It was a staple of life in Roman times when it was called *pulmentum* or *puls*. At that time, polenta was probably made of barley and later of wheat. When corn was brought to Europe from North America, polenta became the dish it is today.

In most northern Italian kitchens, polenta is more than a food, it is a rite. It was made originally in a large copper kettle called a *paiolo*. The kettle was suspended from a thick chain directly over a burning fire. No country kitchen, no matter how poor, was without a fireplace. In the cities, polenta was made on a charcoal- or wood-burning stove. While the woman of the house stirred the cornmeal mixture, the family gathered around, talking and sipping wine.

I remember as a very young girl during wartime, sometimes, somehow, my family would get cornmeal. Then all of us gathered around the stove to watch my mother engaged in the ritual of polenta-making. She would reach inside the

Polenta & Risotto

copper kettle and stir the mixture constantly with a long-handled wooden spoon. And when the golden polenta was poured onto a large, wooden board, it resembled a steaming yellow moon.

Polenta is almost never served by itself. It usually accompanies meat, poultry, fish, cheese or rich sauces. Polenta can be fried, baked, broiled or eaten simply with butter and cheese. When you make polenta, be sure to cook it over medium heat and stir it with a long-handled wooden spoon. The long handle is necessary because polenta will bubble and spit while it thickens. This may leave you with some unwanted tiny burns if you are stirring directly over the kettle.

Polenta is a satisfying food, perfect for cold winter nights, for informal dinners, robust appetites and good company.

Risotto

When I started teaching in California a few years ago, I was amazed at the number of people who had never tasted or heard of *risotto*. Risotto is an important part of northern Italian cuisine and in many regions is more popular than pasta.

Risotto is produced by cooking rice in a particular way, with a technique that is uniquely northern Italian. Italy is the greatest producer of rice in Europe. It is also one of the largest consumers. There are many kinds of risotto, made with the same technique but with different ingredients. Risotto can be made with herbs, vegetables, cheese, sausages, shellfish and many other ingredients. But what is a risotto exactly?

A risotto is rice that is first sautéed briefly with chopped onions in butter. Then enough hot chicken broth is added to cover the rice. The rice is cooked and stirred until the broth is absorbed. Then more broth is added. It is important to stir constantly or the rice will stick. This technique will produce a delicious, creamy risotto with each grain of rice tender yet firm to the bite.

Italian rice, which is thick and short-grained, is perfect for risotto. The best-known exported Italian rice is *arborio*. It is available in Italian groceries and gourmet shops. Short-grain California pearl rice can be used in place of Italian rice. It is similar to the rice used in Italy. Do not select short-grain rice coated with glucose and talc. It is sticky when cooked and is processed for the oriental market. Do not wash short-grain California pearl rice or any rice you use for risotto.

Risotto should be made at the last moment or it will dry out, and reheating makes it become soft and mushy. If you have all the ingredients arranged on a tray and the broth is piping hot, it will be very simple to cook a risotto. A risotto is always served as a first course and is only rarely served with meat. One meat dish it is served with is Veal Shanks Milan-Style, page 114.

In the summer of 1980, my husband and I took a gastronomical tour through northern Italy. Wherever we went, risotto appeared on menus as often as pasta, in incredibly varied and mouthwatering concoctions.

After you have cooked several risottos, I know you will feel as I do, completely hooked on this marvelous northern Italian dish.

Menu

Hot Anchovy Dip, page 14
Basic Polenta, page 62,
with Winter-Style Veal Stew, page 113
Cantaloupes with Marsala Wine,
page 163
Dolcetto or *Barbera

*California wine

Basic Potato Dumplings

Gnocchi di Patate

Transform the humble potato into a melt-in-your-mouth dumpling.

8 medium potatoes, preferably russets　　**1 tablespoon vegetable oil**
1 egg yolk　　**1/4 cup butter**
1 tablespoon salt　　**1/2 cup freshly grated Parmesan cheese**
2 to 2-1/2 cups all-purpose flour

Preheat oven to 350F (175C). With a fork, puncture potatoes in several places. Bake 1 hour or until tender. Remove insides of baked potatoes; discard skins. Mash hot potatoes through a ricer or food mill into a large bowl; let cool slightly. Add egg yolk, 1 tablespoon salt and 2 cups flour; mix well. Put potato mixture on a working surface or wooden board and knead into a ball. Mixture should be soft and pliable and slightly sticky. If it is too sticky, add more flour. Lightly flour working surface and your hands. Break dough into pieces the size of large eggs. Shape pieces into rolls about the thickness of your thumb. Cut rolls into 1-inch pieces. Hold a fork with its tines resting on a work surface at a 45° angle and the inside curve toward you. Take a dumpling roll and press it with your index finger against the outside curve of the fork at the tip end. Quickly slide dumpling up and along the length of the tines, pressing with index finger. Remove finger and let dumpling fall back onto work surface. Grooves made by fork and finger indentation will absorb any sauce served with dumplings. Repeat with remaining dumpling rolls. Arrange dumplings on a floured tray or large plate. Fill a large saucepan two-thirds full with salted water. Bring water to a boil. Add oil and dumplings. When dumplings come to surface of water, cook 10 to 12 seconds. If dumplings remain in water any longer they will absorb water and become too soft. Remove dumplings with a slotted spoon or strainer, draining against side of saucepan. Place in a warm dish. Serve hot with butter and Parmesan cheese or your favorite sauce. Makes 8 servings.

Variation

Potatoes can be boiled instead of baked. Do not puncture potatoes before cooking or they will absorb water, making it necessary to add extra flour to dumpling mixture.

Potato Dumplings with Gorgonzola Sauce

Gnocchi di Patate al Gorgonzola

There is no substitute for the distinctive flavor of Gorgonzola.

Basic Potato Dumplings, above　　**Salt and freshly ground pepper to taste**
1/4 cup butter　　**1 tablespoon vegetable oil**
1/2 cup whipping cream　　**1/3 cup freshly grated Parmesan cheese**
1/4 lb. Gorgonzola cheese, crumbled

Mix and shape Basic Potato Dumplings. Melt butter in a large skillet. When butter foams, add cream and bring to a boil. Add Gorgonzola cheese. Stir and cook 3 to 4 minutes over low heat, until cheese is melted and cream begins to thicken. Season with salt and pepper. Fill a large saucepan two-thirds full with salted water. Bring water to a boil. Add oil and dumplings. When dumplings come to surface of water, cook 10 to 12 seconds. Remove dumplings with a slotted spoon or strainer, draining against side of saucepan. Place dumplings in sauce. Gently stir in Parmesan cheese. Cook 30 to 40 seconds or until dumplings are coated with sauce. Serve immediately. Makes 8 servings.

How to Make Basic Potato Dumplings

1/Add flour to potato mixture.

2/Roll dough and cut into 1-inch pieces.

3/Slide dumpling along tines of a fork.

4/Remove dumplings from pan with a slotted spoon or strainer.

Potato Dumplings with Mushroom Sauce

Gnocchi di Patate con Salsa Rossa i Funghi

Dried, wild Italian mushrooms have a woody fragrance that is unique.

Basic Potato Dumplings, page 58
1 oz. dried wild Italian mushrooms or
   1/4 lb. fresh mushrooms, thinly sliced
1 cup warm water, if using dried mushrooms
2 tablespoons olive oil,
   if using fresh mushrooms
3 tablespoons olive oil
1 large onion, finely chopped

1 (28-oz.) can crushed Italian-style or
   whole tomatoes
Salt and freshly ground pepper to taste
2 tablespoons chopped parsley
2 garlic cloves, finely chopped
1 tablespoon vegetable oil
1/2 cup freshly grated Parmesan cheese

Mix and shape Basic Potato Dumplings. If using dried mushrooms, soak in warm water 20 minutes. Drain mushrooms, reserving liquid. Strain mushroom liquid. Rinse mushrooms under cold running water. Squeeze to remove as much moisture as possible. If using fresh mushrooms, sauté in 2 tablespoons olive oil until golden; set aside. Heat 3 tablespoons olive oil in a medium saucepan. Add onion. Sauté over medium heat until pale yellow. Add soaked and drained dried mushrooms, if using. Sauté 2 to 3 minutes. Press tomatoes through a food mill or sieve, page 161, to remove seeds. Stir tomato pulp into saucepan. Add reserved mushroom liquid. Simmer uncovered 30 to 35 minutes or until sauce reduces to a medium-thick consistency. If using sautéed fresh mushrooms, add to sauce during last 5 minutes of cooking. Season with salt and pepper. Stir in parsley and garlic. Keep sauce on very low heat while dumplings cook. Fill a large saucepan two-thirds full with salted water. Bring water to a boil. Add 1 tablespoon vegetable oil and dumplings. When dumplings come to surface of water, cook 10 to 12 seconds. Remove dumplings with a slotted spoon or strainer, draining against side of saucepan. Place in a warm serving dish. Spoon half the sauce over dumplings and mix gently. Sprinkle with 1/3 cup Parmesan cheese and mix gently. Serve immediately with remaining sauce and Parmesan cheese. Makes 8 servings.

Potato Dumplings with Pesto Sauce

Gnocchi di Patate col Pesto

For perfect dumplings, use starchy potatoes not waxy ones.

Basic Potato Dumplings, page 58
1/2 cup Pesto Sauce, page 159
10 whole walnuts

1 tablespoon vegetable oil
2 tablespoons butter
1/2 cup freshly grated Parmesan cheese

Mix and shape Basic Potato Dumplings. Prepare Pesto Sauce and let stand at room temperature. Chop walnuts very fine. Fill a large saucepan two-thirds full with salted water. Bring water to a boil. Add oil and dumplings. When dumplings come to surface of water, cook 10 to 12 seconds. Remove dumplings with a slotted spoon or strainer, draining against side of saucepan. Place on a warm platter. Add butter, Pesto Sauce and chopped walnuts; mix gently. Serve immediately with Parmesan cheese. Makes 8 servings.

Potato Dumplings Valle D'Aosta-Style

Gnocchi di Patate alla Valdostana

This Piedmont dish is typical of mountain regions. It is robust, hearty and simple.

Basic Potato Dumplings, page 58
1 oz. dried wild Italian mushrooms or
    1/4 lb. fresh mushrooms, thinly sliced
1 cup warm water, if using dried mushrooms
1/4 cup olive oil
3 tablespoons chopped parsley
2 garlic cloves, chopped
Salt and freshly ground pepper to taste

1/2 cup dry white wine
2 tablespoons tomato paste
1/2 cup whipping cream
1 tablespoon vegetable oil
1/3 cup freshly grated Parmesan cheese
1/4 lb. sliced Italian fontina cheese or
    1/2 cup Parmesan cheese

Mix and shape Basic Potato Dumplings. Butter a 13" x 9" baking dish. If using dried mushrooms, soak in warm water 20 minutes. Drain mushrooms, reserving liquid. Strain mushroom liquid. Rinse mushrooms under cold running water. Squeeze to remove as much moisture as possible. Preheat oven to 350F (175C). Heat 1/4 cup olive oil in a large skillet. Add parsley and garlic. Sauté over medium heat 1 minute. Add soaked and drained dried mushrooms or fresh mushrooms and salt and pepper. Sauté until mushrooms are lightly colored. Stir in wine and cook until wine has evaporated. Combine tomato paste and reserved mushroom liquid or, if using fresh mushrooms, 1/2 cup water. Add to skillet. Stir in cream. Simmer 2 to 3 minutes uncovered or until sauce begins to thicken. Fill a large saucepan two-thirds full with salted water. Bring water to a boil. Add 1 tablespoon vegetable oil and dumplings. When dumplings come to surface of water, cook 10 to 12 seconds. Remove dumplings with a slotted spoon or strainer, draining against side of saucepan. Place dumplings in sauce. Stir in 1/3 cup Parmesan cheese and mix gently until dumplings are coated with sauce. Carefully transfer dumplings and sauce to buttered baking dish. Cover with slices of fontina cheese or sprinkle with 1/2 cup Parmesan cheese. Bake 5 to 8 minutes or until cheese is melted. Serve immediately. Makes 8 servings.

Baked Semolina Gnocchi

Gnocchi alla Romana

From Rome, another popular dish that has crossed regional boundaries.

4 cups milk
1-1/2 cups Italian semolina
About 1/4 cup butter

1 cup freshly grated Parmesan cheese
2 egg yolks, lightly beaten
1 tablespoon salt

Butter a 13" x 9" baking dish. Heat milk in a medium saucepan. When milk begins to boil, reduce heat and add semolina very slowly, whisking quickly to avoid lumps. Cook 10 to 15 minutes over medium-low heat, stirring constantly with whisk. Semolina is cooked when it sticks heavily to whisk. Remove pan from heat. Add 3 tablespoons butter, 1/3 cup Parmesan cheese, egg yolks and salt. Mix quickly until well blended. Moisten a work surface or a large dish with water. Pour semolina mixture onto surface and spread it 1/2 inch thick with a wet spatula. Let it cool. Preheat oven to 400F (205C). With a small glass or cookie cutter, cut cooled semolina mixture into 2-inch rounds. Arrange in buttered baking dish, overlapping rounds slightly. Dot with about 1 tablespoon butter and sprinkle with remaining Parmesan cheese. The dish can be prepared to this point and refrigerated a couple of days. Bake 10 to 15 minutes or until golden. For a golden-brown crust, put briefly under preheated broiler. Serve hot. Makes 6 to 8 servings.

Basic Polenta

Polenta

An ancient dish that was and still is a staple in the northern Italian diet.

9 cups water   **3 cups coarse-grain cornmeal**
1 tablespoon salt

Bring water to a boil in a large heavy pot. Add salt and reduce heat until water is simmering. Take cornmeal by the handful and add to water very slowly, controlling the flow to a thin stream through your fingers. To avoid lumps, stir quickly with a long-handled wooden spoon while adding cornmeal. If necessary, stop adding cornmeal from time to time and beat mixture vigorously. Cook, stirring constantly, 20 to 30 minutes. Polenta will become very thick while cooking. It is done when it comes away cleanly from sides of pot. Pour polenta onto a large wooden board or a large platter. Wet your hands and smooth out polenta evenly about 2 inches thick. Let cool 5 to 10 minutes or until polenta solidifies. Cut cooled polenta into slices 1 inch wide and 6 inches long. Place slices in individual dishes. Serve hot, covered with your favorite sauce. Makes 6 to 8 servings.

Variation

Fried Polenta (Polenta Fritta): Prepare Basic Polenta and let cool completely. Cut cooled polenta into slices 2 inches wide and 6 inches long. Pour oil about 1 inch deep in a large skillet. Heat oil until a 1-inch cube of bread turns golden almost immediately. Fry polenta slices on both sides until light golden. Drain on paper towels. Serve hot.

Baked Polenta with Bolognese Meat Sauce

Polenta Pasticciata

A satisfying dish for robust appetites on a cold night with good company.

Basic Polenta, above   **5 to 6 tablespoons butter**
3 to 4 cups Bolognese Meat Sauce, page 160   **1 cup freshly grated Parmesan cheese**

Prepare Basic Polenta and let cool completely. Prepare Bolognese Meat Sauce. Preheat oven to 400F (205C). Butter a 13" x 9" baking dish. Cut cooled polenta into slices 2 inches wide and 6 inches long. Put a third of the sliced polenta in buttered baking dish. Spoon about 1 cup meat sauce over polenta. Dot with about 2 tablespoons butter and sprinkle with 4 to 5 tablespoons Parmesan cheese. Repeat with two more layers of polenta, meat sauce, butter and Parmesan cheese, making 3 layers. Bake 15 to 20 minutes or until cheese is melted. Serve immediately. Makes 6 to 8 servings.

Parmesan cheese should always be grated and never shredded.

How to Make Basic Polenta

1/Gradually add cornmeal to water, stirring constantly.

2/Polenta is cooked when it comes away cleanly from sides of pot.

3/Smooth out polenta with your hands.

4/Cut cooled polenta into slices.

Polenta with Skewered Meat

Polenta con gli Spiedini

In some Italian towns very small birds are used as a delicacy instead of meat in this recipe.

1/2 lb. lean veal shoulder	**2 to 3 medium onions, cut into large pieces**
1/2 lb. pork loin	**Basic Polenta, page 62**
1/2 lb. pancetta, page 6,	**1/4 cup olive oil**
cut into 4 or 5 slices	**Salt and freshly ground pepper to taste**
10 to 12 fresh or dried sage leaves	**1-1/2 cups dry white wine**

Trim all fat from veal and pork. Cut meat into 1-1/2- to 2-inch cubes. Cut pancetta into cubes. On 6 wooden skewers, alternate veal, pancetta, sage, pork and onion; set aside. Prepare Basic Polenta. While polenta cooks, heat oil in a large skillet. Add skewered meat and salt and pepper. Sauté over medium heat 10 minutes, or until meat is lightly browned on all sides. Stir in 3/4 cup wine. Cook uncovered over medium-low heat 15 to 20 minutes, adding more wine as needed. Pour polenta onto a large wooden board or a large platter. Cool 5 minutes. Cut polenta into slices 2 inches wide and 6 inches long. Place 2 slices polenta and 1 skewer of meat on each of 6 individual dishes. Spoon some wine sauce from skillet over each serving. Serve immediately. Makes 6 servings.

Baked Polenta with Butter & Parmesan Cheese

Polenta con Burro e Parmigiano al Forno

Polenta can be prepared ahead and refrigerated. Bring to room temperature before baking.

Basic Polenta, page 62	**1 cup freshly grated Parmesan cheese**
6 tablespoons butter	

Prepare Basic Polenta and let cool completely. Preheat oven to 375F (190C). Butter a large shallow baking dish. Cut cooled polenta into slices 2 inches wide and 6 inches long. Put slices in buttered baking dish. Dot generously with butter and sprinkle with Parmesan cheese. Bake 20 minutes or until cheese is melted. For a golden-brown crust, put briefly under preheated broiler. Serve hot. Makes 6 to 8 servings.

Variation

Polenta with Fontina Cheese (Polenta con la Fontina): Substitute 1/2 lb. sliced Italian fontina cheese for the Parmesan cheese.

Risotto with Spring Vegetables

Risotto Primavera

Use whatever vegetables Spring offers.

5 to 6 cups Chicken Broth, page 20, or
   canned chicken broth
5 tablespoons butter
1 medium onion, finely chopped
2-1/2 cups arborio rice, page 6
1 cup dry white wine
1 cup fresh asparagus tips,
   smallest available

1 cup fresh peas or thawed frozen peas
1/2 cup very finely chopped zucchini
1 cup thinly sliced small white mushrooms
2 tablespoons chopped fresh basil
2 tablespoons chopped parsley
1/2 cup freshly grated Parmesan cheese
Salt to taste

Prepare Chicken Broth. Heat broth in a medium saucepan. Melt 1/4 cup butter in a large saucepan. When butter foams, add onion. Sauté over medium heat until pale yellow. Add rice and mix well. When rice is coated with butter, add wine. Cook, stirring constantly, until wine has evaporated. Stir in 1 or 2 ladles of broth, or enough to cover rice. Stir over medium heat until broth has been absorbed. Continue cooking and stirring rice, adding broth a little at a time, about 10 minutes. Add asparagus tips, peas, zucchini and mushrooms. Cook about 10 minutes longer or until rice is done. Rice should be tender but firm to the bite. Remove pan from heat. Add basil, parsley, 1/3 cup Parmesan cheese and 1 tablespoon butter; mix well. Season with salt. Place in a warm dish. Serve immediately with remaining Parmesan cheese. Makes 6 servings.

Risotto with Dried Mushrooms

Risotto con i Funghi

To get the authentic flavor of this dish, use dried Italian mushrooms.

6 to 8 cups Chicken Broth, page 20, or
   canned chicken broth
1 oz. dried wild Italian mushrooms or
   1/4 lb. fresh mushrooms, thinly sliced
1 cup warm water, if using dried mushrooms
2 tablespoons butter, if using
   fresh mushrooms

5 tablespoons butter
1 medium onion, finely chopped
2-1/2 cups arborio rice, page 6
3/4 cup dry white wine
1/2 cup freshly grated Parmesan cheese
Salt to taste

Prepare Chicken Broth. If using dried mushrooms, soak in warm water 20 minutes. Drain mushrooms, reserving liquid. Strain mushroom liquid. Rinse mushrooms under cold running water. Squeeze to remove as much moisture as possible. If using fresh mushrooms, sauté in 2 tablespoons butter until golden; set aside. Heat broth in a medium saucepan. Melt 1/4 cup butter in a large saucepan. When butter foams, add onion. Sauté over medium heat until pale yellow. Add rice and mix well. When rice is coated with butter, add wine. Cook, stirring constantly, until wine has evaporated. Add drained dried mushrooms and reserved mushroom liquid. Stir in 1 or 2 ladles of broth, or enough to cover rice. Stir over medium heat until broth has been absorbed. Continue cooking and stirring rice, adding broth a little at a time until rice is done, 15 to 20 minutes. Rice should be tender, but firm to the bite. Stir in Parmesan cheese, 1 tablespoon butter and sautéed fresh mushrooms, if using. Season with salt. Place in a warm dish. Serve immediately. Makes 6 servings.

Tricolor Risotto

Risotto Tricolore

One exciting dish with the three colors of the Italian flag and three deliciously different tastes.

8 cups Chicken Broth, page 20, or
  canned chicken broth
6 tablespoons butter
1 large onion, finely chopped
3 cups arborio rice, page 6
1 cup dry white wine

3 tablespoons chopped parsley
1 tablespoon chopped fresh basil
1 tablespoon tomato paste
1 cup freshly grated Parmesan cheese
Salt to taste
Additional Parmesan cheese

Prepare Chicken Broth. Heat broth in a medium saucepan. Melt 3 tablespoons butter in a large saucepan. When butter foams, add onion. Sauté over medium heat until pale yellow. Add rice and mix well. When rice is coated with butter, add wine. Cook, stirring constantly, until wine has evaporated. Stir in 1 or 2 ladles of broth, or enough to cover rice. Stir over medium heat until broth has been absorbed. Continue cooking and stirring rice, adding broth a little at a time, 10 minutes. Divide rice into 3 equal portions. Put 1 portion of rice into each of 2 small saucepans, leaving third portion in original pan. Add parsley and basil to 1 pan, tomato paste to another pan, and nothing to third pan. Continue cooking and stirring rice, adding more broth to each pan when needed. After 5 to 10 minutes when rice is tender but firm to the bite, add 1 tablespoon butter and 1/3 cup Parmesan cheese to each pan. Mix to blend. Season with salt. Arrange rice in a large warm serving dish with white rice in the middle and red and green rice on each side. Serve immediately with additional Parmesan cheese. Makes 6 to 8 servings.

Risotto with Champagne

Risotto allo Champagne

Whoever created this outstanding dish deserves a toast, with champagne, of course.

4 cups Chicken Broth, page 20, or
  canned chicken broth
5 tablespoons butter
1 medium onion, finely chopped

2-1/2 cups arborio rice, page 6
4 cups dry champagne
1 cup freshly grated Parmesan cheese
Salt to taste

Prepare Chicken Broth. Heat broth in a medium saucepan. Melt 1/4 cup butter in a large saucepan. When butter foams, add onion. Sauté over medium heat until pale yellow. Add rice and mix well. When rice is coated with butter, add 1 cup champagne. Cook, stirring constantly, until champagne has evaporated. Stir in 1 or 2 ladles of broth, or enough to cover rice. Stir over medium heat until broth has been absorbed. Continue cooking and stirring rice, adding broth a little at a time, about 10 minutes. During remaining 10 minutes of cooking, add champagne 1 cup at a time instead of broth. Do not add more champagne until previous amount has been absorbed. Rice is done when it is tender but firm to the bite. Stir in 1/2 cup Parmesan cheese and remaining butter. Season with salt. Place in a warm dish. Serve immediately with remaining Parmesan cheese. Makes 6 servings.

Tricolor Risotto

Risotto with Prawns

Risotto con Scampi

Get ahead by preparing Fish Stock and Prawn Sauce in the morning.

Prawn Sauce, see below
Fish Stock, see below
1/4 cup butter
1 medium onion, finely chopped

2-1/2 cups arborio rice, page 6
3/4 cup dry white wine
Pinch of red (cayenne) pepper
Salt to taste

Prawn Sauce:
1 lb. large prawns or shrimp
3 tablespoons olive oil
1/4 cup chopped parsley
3 garlic cloves, finely chopped

2 tablespoons tomato paste
1 cup water
Salt and freshly ground pepper to taste

Fish Stock:
2 lbs. assorted fish for stock
Shells reserved from prawns or shrimp
4 or 5 parsley sprigs
1 garlic clove
1 tablespoon chopped fresh basil or
   1/2 teaspoon dried leaf basil

1 medium onion, sliced
1 carrot, diced
1 celery stalk, diced
1 cup dry white wine
Salt and freshly ground pepper to taste
6 cups water

Prepare Prawn Sauce. Prepare Fish Stock and simmer until ready to use; do not let boil. Melt butter in a medium saucepan. When butter foams, add onion. Sauté over medium heat until pale yellow. Add rice and mix well. When rice is coated with butter, add wine. Cook, stirring constantly, until wine has evaporated. Stir in 1 or 2 ladles of Fish Stock, or enough to cover rice. Stir over medium heat until stock has been absorbed. Continue cooking and stirring rice, adding stock a little at a time until rice is almost done, 10 to 15 minutes. Add Prawn Sauce and mix gently. Cook 2 to 3 minutes longer until rice is tender but firm to the bite. Add a pinch of cayenne and salt to taste. Place in a warm dish. Serve immediately. Makes 6 servings.

Prawn Sauce:

Shell and devein prawns or shrimp, page 81, reserving shells for Fish Stock. Cut prawns or shrimp into thirds. Heat oil in a medium skillet. Sauté parsley and garlic over medium heat. Before garlic begins to color, add prawns or shrimp. Sauté 2 minutes or until they lose pink color. Dilute tomato paste in water and add to prawns. Cook a few minutes longer. Season with salt and pepper and remove from heat.

Fish Stock:

Wash assorted fish well. Place in a medium saucepan. Add reserved shells, parsley, garlic, basil, onion, carrot, celery, wine and salt and pepper. Add water and bring to a boil. Reduce heat and simmer 40 to 50 minutes. Put mixture with liquid through a fine sieve over another medium saucepan.

Canned chicken broth is quite salty. If you are using it, be cautious when seasoning your risotto.

Dante's Risotto

Risotto Dante

Prepare the vegetables ahead and the cooking will be a snap.

1 carrot, halved
1 celery stalk, halved
6 to 8 cups Chicken Broth, page 20, or
    canned chicken broth
6 tablespoons butter
1 medium onion, finely chopped
2-1/2 cups arborio rice, page 6
3/4 cup dry white wine

1/4 lb. small white mushrooms, thinly sliced
1/2 (10-oz.) pkg. thawed frozen spinach,
    finely chopped
2 tablespoons chopped parsley
1/4 lb. prosciutto, page 6, finely chopped
1/3 cup whipping cream
Salt to taste
1 cup freshly grated Parmesan cheese

Fill a small saucepan one-third full with water. Bring water to a boil. Add carrot and celery. Cook over medium heat until barely tender. Finely chop carrot and celery. Prepare Chicken Broth. Heat broth in a medium saucepan. Melt 1/4 cup butter in a large saucepan. When butter foams, add onion. Sauté over medium heat until pale yellow. Add rice and mix well. When rice is coated with butter, add wine. Cook, stirring constantly, until wine has evaporated. Stir in 1 or 2 ladles of broth, or enough to cover rice. Stir over medium heat until broth has been absorbed. Continue cooking and stirring rice, adding broth a little at a time until rice is almost done, 10 to 15 minutes. Melt 1 tablespoon butter in a medium skillet. Add mushrooms. Sauté until golden. Add sautéed mushrooms, spinach, carrot, celery, parsley, prosciutto and cream to rice mixture. Mix well and season with salt. Cook about 5 minutes longer. When rice is tender but firm to the bite, stir in 1/2 cup Parmesan cheese and 1 tablespoon butter. Place in a warm dish. Serve immediately with remaining Parmesan cheese. Makes 6 servings.

Risotto Milan-Style

Risotto alla Milanese

This golden risotto and Veal Shanks Milan-Style, page 114, are traditionally served together.

6 to 8 cups Chicken Broth, page 20, or
    canned chicken broth
5 tablespoons butter
1 medium onion, finely chopped
2-1/2 cups arborio rice, page 6

3/4 cup dry white wine
1/2 teaspoon saffron
1/2 cup freshly grated Parmesan cheese
Salt to taste
Additional Parmesan cheese

Prepare Chicken Broth. Heat broth in a medium saucepan. Melt 1/4 cup butter in a large saucepan. When butter foams, add onion. Sauté over medium heat until pale yellow. Add rice and mix well. When rice is coated with butter, add wine. Cook, stirring constantly, until wine has evaporated. Stir in 1 or 2 ladles of broth, or enough to cover rice. Stir over medium heat until broth has been absorbed. Continue cooking and stirring rice, adding broth a little at a time until rice is done, 15 to 20 minutes. Rice should be tender but firm to the bite. In a small bowl, dissolve saffron in a little hot broth and add to rice mixture. Stir in 1/2 cup Parmesan cheese and 1 tablespoon butter. Season with salt. Place in a warm dish. Serve immediately with additional Parmesan cheese. Makes 6 servings.

Risotto with Cream & Cheese Sauce

Risotto alla Crema di Formaggio

A variation on a classic theme. Simply outstanding and outstandingly simple.

**6 to 8 cups Chicken Broth, page 20, or
  canned chicken broth**
5 tablespoons butter
1 medium onion, finely chopped
2-1/2 cups arborio rice, page 6

3/4 cup dry white wine
3/4 cup whipping cream
1/2 cup freshly grated Parmesan cheese
Salt to taste

Prepare Chicken Broth. Heat broth in a medium saucepan. Melt 1/4 cup butter in a large saucepan. When butter foams, add onion. Sauté over medium heat until pale yellow. Add rice and mix well. When rice is coated with butter, add wine. Cook, stirring constantly, until wine has evaporated. Stir in 1 or 2 ladles of broth, or enough to cover rice. Stir over medium heat until broth has been absorbed. Continue cooking and stirring rice, adding broth a little at a time until rice is almost done, 10 to 15 minutes. Bring cream to a boil in a small saucepan. Add Parmesan cheese, mixing quickly. When cream is well blended with cheese, add to rice. Cook 2 or 3 minutes or until rice is tender but firm to the bite. Season with salt. Stir in remaining butter. Place in a warm dish. Serve immediately. Makes 6 servings.

Variation

Risotto with Parmesan Cheese (Risotto alla Parmigiana): Omit cream. Stir 1/2 cup freshly grated Parmesan cheese and 1 tablespoon butter into cooked rice.

Pumpkin Risotto

Risotto con la Zucca

Pumpkin gives a delicate taste to this risotto from Lombardy.

**6 cups Chicken Broth, page 20, or
  canned chicken broth**
1 lb. pumpkin
1/4 cup butter

1 medium onion, finely chopped
2 cups arborio rice, page 6
1/2 cup freshly grated Parmesan cheese
Additional Parmesan cheese

Prepare Chicken Broth. Heat broth in a medium saucepan. Peel pumpkin and discard seeds. Cut pumpkin into very small pieces. Melt 3 tablespoons butter in a large saucepan. When butter foams, add onion. Sauté over medium heat until pale yellow. Add pumpkin and mix well. Add 1 or 2 ladles of broth, or enough to cover pumpkin mixture. Cook uncovered over medium heat 10 minutes. Stir in rice and 1 cup broth. Continue cooking and stirring rice, adding broth a little at a time until rice is done, 15 to 20 minutes. Rice should be tender but firm to the bite. Add 1/2 cup Parmesan cheese and 1 tablespoon butter; mix well. Place in a warm dish. Serve immediately with additional Parmesan cheese. Makes 4 servings.

How to Make Risotto with Parmesan Cheese

1/Add broth a little at a time while rice is cooking.

2/Add Parmesan cheese and butter to cooked rice.

Risotto with Asparagus Tips

Risotto con Punte di Asparagi

Make this dish in the summer months when asparagus is at its peak.

6 cups Chicken Broth, page 20, or
   canned chicken broth
1-1/2 lbs. asparagus, smallest available
6 tablespoons butter
1 medium onion, finely chopped
2-1/2 cups arborio rice, page 6

1/2 cup dry white wine
1/3 cup whipping cream
1/2 cup freshly grated Parmesan cheese
Salt to taste
Additional Parmesan cheese

Prepare Chicken Broth. Clean asparagus and cut off tips. Reserve stalks for another use. Heat broth in a medium saucepan. Melt 1/4 cup butter in a large saucepan. When butter foams, add onion. Sauté over medium heat until pale yellow. Add rice and mix well. When rice is coated with butter, add wine. Cook, stirring constantly, until wine has evaporated. Stir in 1 or 2 ladles of broth, or enough to cover rice. Stir over medium heat until broth has been absorbed. Add more broth as liquid is absorbed. After 10 minutes add asparagus tips. Continue cooking and stirring rice, adding broth a little at a time until rice is done, about 10 minutes. Rice should be tender but firm to the bite. Add cream, 1/2 cup Parmesan cheese and remaining butter; mix gently. Season with salt. Place in a warm dish. Serve immediately with additional Parmesan cheese. Makes 6 servings.

Italy is a long, thin peninsula with the Adriatic Sea to the east and the Mediterranean Sea to the west. No wonder Italians are great fish lovers! But if you leave the Italian seacoasts and go inland, you will find fish consumption is less than you would expect from a country practically surrounded by water.

I was born in Emilia-Romagna. The Emilia side is inland, the Romagna side has a seacoast. In my family, fish was eaten maybe two or three times a month. But I would readily get into a car with family or friends and drive to the coastal town of Rimini to eat the fresh catch of the day. Everybody knew the best fish was to be had at the coast.

Restaurants of the area specialized in excellently prepared fish. Inside these restaurants, fish was generally displayed on a long table with some fish still alive inside large containers of water. You would choose the fish you preferred, then 10 minutes later it would arrive on your plate, broiled, fried, or poached.

What could be better than a fresh batch of shrimp coated lightly with a parsley-garlic mixture and broiled for the briefest time? Or a large pot

Menu

Tagliatelle with Scallops
& Cream Sauce, page 36
Fish in Foil, page 74
Buttered Carrots, page 141
Cold Zabaglione, page 177,
with Fresh Strawberries
Pinot Grigio or *Pinot Blanc

*California wine

Shellfish

of clams, simmered in a fresh tomato and herb sauce and served over pasta? Or fresh sole, cooked in a butter-lemon sauce? Italians do not camouflage fish under rich, heavy sauces, but complement them with delicate flavors.

In addition to the marvelously simple fish dishes, every coastal town in Italy has its own fish soup. Whether it is *Broeto* from Venice, *Cacciucco* from Leghorn, or *Ciuppin* from Liguria, each region claims its fish soup is the best.

The first thing to do when buying fish is to make sure it is fresh. If fish has the head still on, look at the eyes. They should be bright and rounded, not sunken. Look for a moist, shiny skin. The body should be firm and compact, not mushy. Fish should have a fresh ocean smell. If you don't plan to use fresh fish the same day, place the wrapped fish in a plastic bag and seal it tightly. Put the fish in the coldest part of your refrigerator immediately. Use it within two days.

Frozen fish tends to lose part of its precious moisture as it thaws. This leaves the fish mushy. When you use frozen fish, thaw it in the refrigerator for several hours or overnight. Don't leave fish at room temperature or it will thaw too quickly and some of its juices will be lost.

Fish and shellfish need only a short cooking time. When in doubt, undercook fish, rather than overcooking it. If the flesh flakes easily when pierced with a fork or knife, fish is cooked. Shellfish is cooked when it is opaque all the way through. If the center of shellfish is transparent, it should be cooked longer.

Fish is high in protein, minerals and vitamins. It is also low in calories. Unfortunately the price of fish today is considerably higher than it used to be. One way to save money is to buy when fish is in season and plentiful. Many dishes in this chapter can be used as appetizers or main courses. Some dishes, like Prawns with Tomato & Garlic, can also become a divine sauce for pasta. Serve fish accompanied by chilled white wine and you will have a perfect union.

I hope the recipes in this chapter will encourage you to try simple but exciting ways to cook fish the northern Italian way.

Salt Cod Bologna-Style

Baccalá alla Bolognese

Dried salt cod can be found in Italian and other ethnic markets.

1-1/2 lbs. dried salt cod fillets
1/2 cup all-purpose flour
1/3 cup olive oil
3 garlic cloves, chopped

1/4 cup chopped parsley
Salt and freshly ground pepper to taste
Juice of 3 lemons

Cut fish into large serving pieces, about 4 inches square. Place in a large bowl; add enough cold water to cover. Let stand 24 hours, changing water several times. Dry fish with paper towels. Spread flour on aluminum foil. Coat fish with flour. Heat oil in a large skillet. Add fish. Cook over medium heat 5 to 6 minutes on each side or until golden. Sprinkle with garlic and parsley and season with salt and pepper. Gently place cod on a warm platter. Add lemon juice to skillet. Deglaze by stirring to dissolve fish juices attached to bottom of skillet. Spoon sauce over fish. Serve immediately. Makes 4 to 6 servings.

Fish in Foil

Pesce al Cartoccio

Fish cooked in foil or parchment paper retains all its flavor and moisture.

**1 (3- to 3-1/2-lb.) sea bass,
striped bass or red snapper, cleaned
3 garlic cloves, finely chopped
Leaves from 2 sprigs fresh rosemary or
2 teaspoons dried rosemary**

**2 tablespoons chopped parsley
Juice of 1 lemon
1/3 cup olive oil
Salt and freshly ground pepper to taste
Lemon wedges**

Preheat oven to 400F (205C). Wash fish thoroughly under cold running water. Dry with paper towels. In a small bowl, combine garlic, rosemary, parsley, lemon juice, oil and salt and pepper. Cut a large piece of aluminum foil or parchment paper to twice the size of fish. Lay fish on foil or paper. Fill fish with half the garlic-rosemary mixture. Spread remaining mixture over top of fish. Fold foil or paper over fish. Pleat edges to seal tightly. Place in a baking dish. Bake 10 minutes per pound, 30 to 35 minutes. Place fish on a board and open foil or paper. Gently remove skin. Cut top half of fish lengthwise into 2 servings and place on plates. Lift off backbone and any loose bones from fish. Divide remaining fish into 2 servings and place on plates. Spoon fish juices over each serving. Season lightly with salt and pepper. Serve with lemon wedges. Makes 4 servings.

Variation

Trout in Foil (Trota al Cartoccio): Substitute 4 trout that have been cleaned but their heads and tails left on. Wrap each trout individually. Let guests unwrap their fish at the table.

How to Make Trout in Foil

1/Cut top half of fish lengthwise into 2 pieces.

2/Lift off backbone and any loose bones from fish.

Fresh Tuna Fish Genoa-Style

Tonno alla Genovese

You won't recognize this as the same fish you have had in cans.

1 oz. dried wild Italian mushrooms	1 teaspoon all-purpose flour
3/4 cup warm water	1 cup dry white wine
3 tablespoons olive oil	4 fresh tuna fish steaks, 3/4 inch thick
3 tablespoons chopped parsley	Salt and freshly ground pepper to taste
2 garlic cloves, chopped	1 tablespoon butter
2 or 3 flat anchovy fillets	Juice of 1 lemon

Soak mushrooms in warm water 20 minutes. Drain, reserving liquid. Strain mushroom liquid. Rinse mushrooms under cold running water. Squeeze to remove as much moisture as possible. Heat oil in a large skillet. Add mushrooms, parsley, garlic, anchovies and flour. Stir over medium heat until garlic begins to color. Stir in wine. When wine is reduced by half, add tuna steaks. Season with salt and pepper. Cover and cook about 5 minutes. Gently turn tuna and cook 3 to 5 minutes or until fish can be flaked. Place fish on a warm platter. Keep warm in oven. Add reserved mushroom liquid to skillet with butter and lemon juice. Cook over high heat until sauce has a medium-thick consistency. Spoon sauce over tuna. Serve immediately. Makes 4 servings.

Fried Sole Fillets

Filetti di Sogliola Dorati

Sole fillets, breaded and fried lightly in butter, retain all their moisture and delicate flavor.

1/2 cup all-purpose flour	4 sole fillets
1 cup dry unflavored breadcrumbs	3 tablespoons butter
2 eggs	1 tablespoon olive oil
Salt and freshly ground pepper to taste	Lemon wedges

Spread flour and breadcrumbs separately on 2 pieces of aluminum foil. Beat eggs with salt and pepper in a medium bowl. Coat fish with flour, shaking off excess. Dip in beaten eggs, then coat with breadcrumbs. Press breadcrumbs onto fish with the palms of your hands. Let coated fish stand 10 to 15 minutes. Melt butter with oil in a large skillet. When butter foams, add fish. Cook over medium heat 3 to 4 minutes on each side or until golden. Place fish on a warm platter. Garnish with lemon wedges. Serve immediately. Makes 4 servings.

Marinated Sole Venetian-Style

Sogliola in Saor

A very old Venetian dish with an unusual combination of ingredients.

1/3 cup raisins	2 large onions, thinly sliced
1/2 cup all-purpose flour	1/3 cup white wine vinegar
6 sole fillets	1 tablespoon sugar
1/2 cup olive oil	1/3 cup pine nuts
Salt to taste	1 tablespoon chopped parsley

Put raisins in a small bowl. Add enough warm water to cover. Let stand 20 minutes, then drain. Spread flour on aluminum foil. Coat fillets with flour, shaking off excess. Heat 1/3 cup oil in a large skillet. Add fish. Cook over medium heat 2 to 3 minutes on each side or until golden. Drain on paper towels. Season with salt. Heat remaining oil in a medium skillet. Add onions. Sauté over medium heat until pale yellow. Increase heat and add vinegar. Bring to a boil and cook about 1 minute, stirring constantly. Add sugar, raisins and pine nuts. Cook 1 minute longer. Arrange fish in a single layer in a large shallow dish. Spoon onion sauce over fish and sprinkle with parsley. Cover dish. Refrigerate at least 24 hours. Serve at room temperature. Makes 6 servings.

Sole Fillets with Cream Sauce

Sogliola alla Panna

An elegant dish that requires little time but has to be made at the last moment.

1/2 cup all-purpose flour	**1/3 cup brandy**
4 sole fillets	**1/2 cup whipping cream**
Salt and white pepper to taste	**2 tablespoons chopped parsley**
3 tablespoons butter	**1 garlic clove, chopped**
1 tablespoon olive oil	

Spread flour on aluminum foil. Coat fillets with flour, shaking off excess. Season with salt and pepper. Melt butter with oil in a large skillet. When butter foams, add fish. Cook over medium heat 2 to 3 minutes on each side or until golden. Gently place fish on a warm platter. Keep warm in oven. Add brandy to skillet. Deglaze by stirring to dissolve fish juices attached to bottom of skillet. Add cream, parsley and garlic. Cook and stir 1 to 2 minutes or until sauce has a medium-thick consistency. Taste and adjust for seasoning, then spoon sauce over fish. Serve immediately. Makes 4 servings.

Baked Sole Fillets

Filetti di Sogliola Delicati al Forno

Put the completed dish under the broiler briefly for a rich golden color.

8 sole fillets	**Basic White Sauce, page 158, made with**
2 tablespoons butter	**1 cup milk**
Salt and white pepper to taste	**2 tablespoons chopped parsely**
1/2 cup dry sherry	

Preheat oven 375F (190C). Butter an 11'' x 7'' baking dish. Fold sole fillets in half and arrange in buttered baking dish. Melt butter. Pour a little melted butter over each fillet. Season with salt and pepper. Pour sherry into baking dish. Cover dish with aluminum foil. Bake 10 minutes. Prepare Basic White Sauce. Remove fish from oven. Spoon fish juices from baking dish into white sauce. Stir until blended. Add parsley. Taste and adjust for seasoning. Spoon sauce over fish. Return to oven and bake uncovered 10 minutes longer. Serve hot. Makes 8 servings.

Broiled Shrimp & Scallops

Scampi e Cape Sante alla Griglia

Whether you serve this dish as an appetizer or main course, it is equally sensational.

1 lb. medium shrimp
1 lb. scallops
1/2 cup olive oil
1/3 cup chopped parsley

3 garlic cloves, finely chopped
1/2 cup dry unflavored breadcrumbs
Salt and freshly ground pepper to taste
Lemon wedges

Shell and devein shrimp, page 81. Wash shrimp and scallops under cold running water. Pat dry with paper towels. In a large bowl, combine oil, parsley, garlic, breadcrumbs and salt and pepper. Add shrimp and scallops to mixture. Mix until well coated. Let stand 1 hour. Preheat broiler. Remove shrimp and scallops from marinade. Gently press some extra breadcrumb mixture onto shrimp and scallops. Place alternately on 4 to 6 metal skewers. Put skewers under hot broiler. Broil 2 minutes or until golden. Turn skewers over and broil on the other side 2 minutes or until golden. Serve immediately with lemon wedges. Makes 4 to 6 servings.

Scallops Venetian-Style

Cape Sante alla Veneziana

The Italian way with seafood is remarkable for its simplicity.

1-1/2 lbs. scallops
1/4 cup olive oil
2 garlic cloves, chopped

2 tablespoons chopped parsley
Salt and freshly ground pepper to taste
Juice of 2 lemons

Wash scallops under cold running water. Pat dry with paper towels. Heat oil in a medium skillet. Add scallops, garlic and parsley. Season with salt and pepper. Cook over medium-low heat 5 to 6 minutes or until golden. Stir several times during cooking. Add lemon juice and mix well. Place on a warm platter. Serve immediately. Makes 4 to 6 servings.

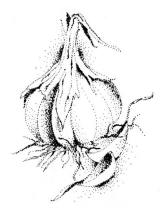

Broiled Shrimp & Scallops and Mixed Salad, page 149

Prawns with Garlic & Tomato

Scampi con Aglio e Pomodoro

You can find many different kinds of scampi in Italy.

16 large prawns or 20 medium shrimp
1 cup canned crushed Italian-style or
   whole tomatoes
1/4 cup olive oil
4 garlic cloves, finely chopped

3/4 cup dry white wine
1 tablespoon chopped parsley
Salt and freshly ground pepper to taste
8 thick slices Italian bread

Shell and devein prawns or shrimp, opposite, and wash under cold running water. Pat dry with paper towels. Press tomatoes through a food mill or sieve, page 161, to remove seeds. Heat oil in a large skillet. Add garlic and prawns or shrimp. Sauté over medium heat until garlic and prawns or shrimp are lightly colored. Stir in wine. When wine is reduced by half, add tomato pulp. Cook 2 to 3 minutes if using shrimp and 4 to 6 minutes if using prawns. Stir several times during cooking. Add parsley and season with salt and pepper. Toast bread until golden on both sides. Place prawn or shrimp mixture in a warm dish. Serve immediately with toasted bread. Makes 4 servings.

Prawns Peasant-Style

Scampi alla Contadina

If you have any sauce left over, cut prawns into small pieces and serve over pasta.

4 medium tomatoes
1-1/2 lbs. prawns
1/4 cup olive oil
3 or 4 garlic cloves, chopped
3 tablespoons dry unflavored breadcrumbs
About 1 cup dry white wine

2 tablespoons chopped parsley
1/3 small red or green hot pepper,
   finely chopped, or small pinch
   red (cayenne) pepper
Salt to taste

Peel, seed and dice tomatoes, page 42. Shell and devein prawns, opposite, and wash under cold running water. Pat dry with paper towels. Heat oil in a large skillet. Add garlic. Sauté over medium heat until garlic begins to color. Add breadcrumbs and mix well. Stir in wine. When wine is reduced by half, add diced tomatoes, parsley, hot pepper and prawns. Season with salt and mix well. Cook uncovered over medium heat 8 to 10 minutes, stirring a few times during cooking. If sauce looks too dry, add a little more wine. Place in a warm dish. Serve immediately. Makes 4 to 6 servings.

How to Shell & Devein Shrimp or Prawns

1/Pull away shell from shrimp or prawn.

2/Make a shallow cut along length of shrimp or prawn. Remove dark vein from opening.

Fried Prawns

Gamberoni Fritti

A crisp green salad and chilled white wine are all you need to complete a light dinner.

16 large prawns or 20 medium shrimp	**4 garlic cloves**
2 eggs	**Salt to taste**
1/2 cup all-purpose flour	**Lemon wedges**
Oil for frying	

Shell and devein prawns or shrimp, above, and wash under cold running water. Pat dry with paper towels. Beat eggs in a medium bowl. Spread flour on aluminum foil. Coat prawns or shrimp with flour, shaking off excess. Pour oil 1 inch deep in a medium skillet or saucepan. Heat oil until a 1-inch cube of bread turns golden brown almost immediately. Add garlic. Sauté garlic until golden, then remove with a slotted spoon. Dip prawns or shrimp into beaten eggs. Using slotted spoon, lower prawns or shrimps into hot oil. Sauté over medium heat until golden. Remove from skillet with slotted spoon. Drain on paper towels. Season with salt. Arrange prawns or shrimp on a warm platter. Garnish with lemon wedges. Serve hot. Makes 4 servings.

Fish Soup Leghorn-Style

Cacciucco alla Livornese

Every coastal region in Italy has its fish soup. The goodness and aroma of the sea goes into each one.

7 or 8 medium tomatoes
1/4 lb. ling cod
1/4 lb. halibut
1/4 lb. striped bass
1/4 lb. red snapper
1/4 lb. squid
1/4 lb. medium shrimp
1/4 lb. scallops
1 lb. small clams
1/3 cup olive oil
1 medium onion, finely chopped

1 carrot, finely chopped
1 celery stalk, finely chopped
3 tablespoons chopped parsley
3 garlic cloves, chopped
1/3 small red or green hot pepper,
    finely chopped
About 1 cup dry white wine
Salt to taste
12 to 16 slices Italian bread
2 garlic cloves

Peel, seed and dice tomatoes, page 42. Wash all fish thoroughly under cold running water. Cut into large pieces. Cut squid head off below the eye and discard. Slice squid tentacles into small pieces. Clean inside squid stomach by removing everything under cold running water, then cut into rings. Shell and devein shrimp, page 81. Wash shrimp and scallops under cold running water. Scrub clams with a brush and rinse thoroughly. Place clams in a pot of cold water and change water several times. Ingredients can be prepared several hours ahead and left in a pot of cold water until ready to use. Heat oil in a large saucepan or casserole. Add onion, carrot, celery, 2 tablespoons parsley, 2 chopped garlic cloves and hot pepper. Sauté over medium heat until vegetables are lightly browned. Add squid and wine. Cook 5 minutes. Add diced tomatoes and season with salt. Reduce heat and cook uncovered 5 minutes, stirring occasionally. Add prepared fish and cook 5 minutes longer. Add prepared shrimp, scallops and clams. Cook covered 5 minutes longer. Sprinkle remaining parsley and 1 chopped garlic clove over fish. Stir in a little more wine if sauce is too thick. Remove from heat. Toast bread until golden on both sides. Cut 2 garlic cloves in half. Rub toasted bread with cut garlic. Place 2 slices toasted bread in each soup bowl. Ladle fish soup over toast. Serve immediately. Makes 6 to 8 servings.

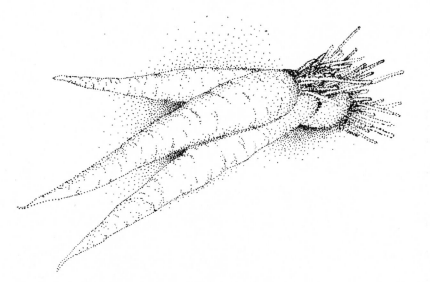

Trout with Green Mayonnaise

Trota con Maionese Verde

If you don't have a fish poacher use a large roasting or broiling pan.

1-1/2 cups Mayonnaise, page 157
2 tablespoons Green Sauce, page 159
4 trout, cleaned, heads and tails left on
2 cups dry white wine
1 medium onion, chopped

1 carrot, chopped
1 celery stalk, cut into 3 pieces
3 or 4 sprigs parsley
Juice of 1 lemon
Salt and freshly ground pepper to taste

Prepare Mayonnaise. Prepare Green Sauce. Combine Mayonnaise and Green Sauce in a medium bowl. Wash fish and place in a fish poacher. Add enough hot water to cover. Add wine, onion, carrot, celery, parsley, lemon and salt and pepper. Bring to a boil. Cover and reduce heat. Simmer 10 to 12 minutes. Fish is cooked when skin becomes lighter in color and flesh is firm to the touch and flaky. Remove fish from liquid and cut off heads and tails. Remove skin by lifting it gently away from fish. Place fish on serving plates. Serve with green mayonnaise. Makes 4 servings.

Wrap fish in cheesecloth so it will be easier to place in and remove from pan.

Game &

Most Italians are not great red-meat lovers, but give them white, tender meat, and their enthusiasm and culinary skills will perform wonders.

Most types of poultry and game, like chicken, pheasant and rabbit, have been used in Italian cooking for centuries. Turkey is the exception. It was introduced into Europe from North America by the Spaniards in the early sixteenth century.

In some northern regions, like Lombardy and Piedmont, turkey is served at Christmas. The bird is roasted and stuffed with a mixture of chestnuts, sausage, truffles, apples and prunes.

If turkey is relatively new on Italian tables, chicken is not. The chickens of ancient Rome were kept because they produced eggs. They were so scrawny that they were not considered good enough to eat. Eventually the Romans learned how to fatten chickens. They have been avidly devoured ever since. When we were children, I would often go with my brother and sister to visit an aunt who had a farm 20 miles outside

Menu

Bean Soup Veneto-Style, page 26
Roast Rabbit, page 86
Roasted Potato Balls, page 140
Mixed Salad, page 149
Cheese Fritters, page 165
Taurasi, Chianti Classico Riserva,
or *Light Cabernet Sauvignon

*California wine

Poultry

Bologna. Besides climbing trees and rolling in the grass, we also chased chickens, turkeys and ducks. We would return home loaded with fresh eggs, white flour, country bread and a few live chickens. I still maintain that those were the best chickens my mother ever prepared.

The number of chicken dishes in the Italian repertory is staggering. A chicken can be broiled, baked, stewed or cooked on a spit. It can also be cooked with innumerable sauces, changing it to fit either a simple or an elaborate menu.

Chicken breasts can be used in many ways. They can be breaded and sautéed. They can be pounded and treated like veal scaloppine. Marsala wine combined with cream to make a rich sauce can turn chicken breasts into an elegant meal.

One favorite Italian way of cooking chicken is pan-roasting. Using this method, the meat juices are sealed by browning the chicken in butter or oil. Then the heat is reduced and a little liquid is added to prevent the chicken from drying out.

Chicken is a particularly good buy. It is an excellent source of protein, vitamin B and iron. In selecting a chicken or turkey, look for a plump bird with firm meat. The skin should be moist but not sticky. Smell the bird. Any unpleasant odor should deter you from buying it.

In some regions of Italy, rabbit and pheasant are very popular. Rabbit has very little fat. It is delicate in taste with a particular sweet flavor. Rabbit can be cooked in many ways. My favorite method is to braise it in a rich tomato-based sauce. Rabbit cooked this way will retain all its tenderness and moisture. A few slices of steaming *polenta* make the perfect accompaniment.

Wild pheasant has to be caught, hung, plucked, marinated and cleaned thoroughly before cooking. But the readily available domestic pheasant can be cleaned and cooked much like a chicken. Pheasant, like rabbit, can be fried, roasted or braised. In some regions, pheasant is also cooked on an open spit, basted with lard. However you choose to cook pheasant, serve it with polenta to make an incomparable partnership.

Pan-Roasted Chicken

Pollo Arrosto in Padella

Pan-roasting is typically Italian and helps meat to retain its moisture.

1 (2-1/2- to 3-1/2-lb.) frying chicken,
   cut into serving pieces
2 tablespoons butter
2 tablespoons olive oil
3 garlic cloves, crushed

2 sprigs fresh rosemary or
   1 teaspoon dried rosemary
Salt and freshly ground pepper to taste
1/2 cup dry white wine

Wash and dry chicken thoroughly. Melt butter with oil in a large skillet. When butter foams, add chicken pieces, garlic and rosemary. Brown chicken on all sides over medium heat. Season with salt and pepper. Add wine. When wine is reduced by half, partially cover skillet. Cook over medium heat 30 to 40 minutes or until chicken is tender. Place chicken on a warm platter. If sauce looks dry, stir in a little more wine. If sauce is too thin, increase heat and boil uncovered until it reaches desired thickness. Remove most of fat from sauce. Taste and adjust sauce for seasoning, then spoon over chicken. Serve immediately. Makes 4 servings.

Roast Rabbit

Coniglio Arrosto

Rabbit marinated in oil and vinegar becomes especially tender and flavorful.

1 (2-1/2- to 3-lb.) rabbit
Leaves from 1 sprig fresh rosemary or
  1 teaspoon dried rosemary
4 fresh sage leaves or
  1/2 teaspoon rubbed sage

2 garlic cloves
10 juniper berries
Salt and freshly ground pepper to taste
4 to 5 tablespoons white wine vinegar
1/2 cup olive oil

Cut rabbit into serving pieces or ask the butcher to do so. Wash and dry thoroughly. Coarsely chop rosemary, sage and garlic together. Crush juniper berries; add to rosemary mixture. Rub rabbit pieces with rosemary-juniper mixture. Season with salt and pepper. Put rabbit pieces into a large bowl. Add vinegar and oil. Let stand 3 to 4 hours, turning meat a few times. Place rabbit and marinade in a large heavy casserole. Bring to a boil. Reduce heat and cover casserole. Simmer 40 to 50 minutes, stirring a few times during cooking. Increase heat to medium-high. Cook uncovered 10 to 15 minutes or until rabbit is tender and only a few tablespoons of sauce remain. Place rabbit on a warm platter. Taste and adjust sauce for seasoning, then spoon over rabbit. Serve immediately. Makes 4 to 6 servings.

Rabbit with Wine & Vegetables

Coniglio alla Reggiana

Nothing was ever left on our plates after my mother served this special dish.

1 (2-1/2- to 3-lb.) rabbit
1-1/2 cups canned crushed Italian-style or
  whole tomatoes
1/4 cup butter
1/4 lb. pancetta, page 6,
  cut into 4 slices and diced
2 large onions, thinly sliced

1 carrot, finely chopped
1 celery stalk, finely chopped
3/4 cup dry white wine
Salt and freshly ground pepper to taste
2 tablespoons chopped parsley
2 garlic cloves, chopped

Cut rabbit into serving pieces or ask the butcher to do so. Wash and dry thoroughly. Press tomatoes through a food mill or sieve, page 161, to remove seeds. Melt butter in a large heavy casserole. When butter foams, add rabbit pieces, pancetta, onion, carrot and celery. Cook over medium heat until rabbit is golden on all sides. Stir in wine. When wine has evaporated, add tomato pulp. Season with salt and pepper. Cover casserole and cook over medium heat 30 to 40 minutes. Stir mixture a few times during cooking. Add parsley and garlic. Cook covered 20 to 25 minutes longer or until meat is tender. Place rabbit on a warm platter. Taste and adjust sauce for seasoning, then spoon over rabbit. Serve hot. Makes 4 to 6 servings.

Pheasant with Mushrooms

Fagiano con i Funghi

Serve this with a steaming hot dish of Polenta, page 62.

1 oz. dried wild Italian mushrooms or
   1/4 lb. fresh mushrooms, thinly sliced
1 cup warm water, if using dried mushrooms
2 tablespoons olive oil, if using
   fresh mushrooms
1 (2-1/2- to 3-lb.) domestic pheasant
3 tablespoons butter
2 tablespoons olive oil
Salt and freshly ground pepper to taste
1/3 cup brandy

1 carrot, finely chopped
1 medium onion, finely chopped
1 celery stalk, finely chopped
3 fresh sage leaves or
   1/2 teaspoon rubbed sage
2 tablespoons chopped parsley
1/3 cup dry Marsala wine or port
2 cups canned crushed Italian-style or
   whole tomatoes

If using dried mushrooms, soak in warm water 20 minutes. Drain mushrooms, reserving liquid. Strain mushroom liquid. Rinse mushrooms under cold running water. Squeeze to remove as much moisture as possible. If using fresh mushrooms, sauté in 2 tablespoons oil or until golden; set aside. Divide pheasant into 4 pieces. Wash and dry pheasant pieces thoroughly. Melt butter with 2 tablespoons oil in a large heavy casserole. When butter foams, add pheasant. Brown on all sides over medium heat. Season with salt and pepper. Add brandy. When brandy is reduced by half, add carrot, onion, celery, sage and parsley. Sauté until lightly browned. Add Marsala or port and cook 1 to 2 minutes longer. Press tomatoes through a food mill or sieve, page 161, to remove seeds. Stir tomato pulp into casserole. Cover casserole and reduce heat. If using dried mushrooms, add to casserole with reserved liquid. Simmer 50 to 60 minutes or until pheasant is tender. Turn meat occasionally during cooking. Cook uncovered 10 to 15 minutes longer. If using sautéed fresh mushrooms, add to sauce during last 5 minutes of cooking. Place pheasant on a warm platter. Taste and adjust sauce for seasoning, then spoon over pheasant. Serve immediately. Makes 4 servings.

Pheasant with Gin & Juniper Berries

Fagiano al Gin e Bacche di Ginepro

Gin and juniper berries give a distinctive flavor to this succulent dish.

1-1/2 cups dry white wine
2 tablespoons juniper berries
1 teaspoon black peppercorns
1 (2-1/2- to 3-lb.) domestic pheasant
Salt and freshly ground pepper to taste
6 tablespoons butter
2 carrots, finely chopped
1 medium onion, finely chopped

2 garlic cloves, finely chopped
1/4 lb. pancetta, page 6,
   cut into 4 slices and diced
Grated zest of 1 lemon
1 tablespoon all-purpose flour
1/3 cup gin
Juice of 1 lemon

Combine wine, juniper berries and peppercorns in a small bowl. Let stand 2 hours. Wash and dry pheasant thoroughly. Season with salt and pepper inside bird and outside. Tie firmly with kitchen twine to retain its shape. Melt 5 tablespoons butter in a large heavy casserole. When butter foams, add pheasant breast-side down. Brown on all sides over medium heat. Add carrots, onion, garlic and pancetta. Sauté until lightly browned. Drain juniper berries and peppercorns, reserving wine. Crush juniper berries and peppercorns. Pour wine over pheasant. When wine is reduced by half, add juniper berries, peppercorns and lemon zest. Cover casserole. Cook over medium heat 1-1/2 hours or until pheasant is tender. Place pheasant on a cutting board. Combine 1 tablespoon butter and flour and work into a small ball. Raise heat. Stir gin and lemon juice into casserole. Add butter-flour ball and mix until well blended, about 1 minute. Press sauce through a sieve into a warm bowl. Cut pheasant into 4 pieces. Arrange on a warm platter. Taste and adjust sauce for seasoning, then spoon over pheasant. Serve immediately. Makes 4 servings.

Adding a butter-flour ball to a thin sauce will thicken it and make it creamy smooth.

Stuffed Chicken Breasts

Involtini di Pollo con Prosciutto e Formaggio

Fontina or Parmesan cheese paired with sage makes an intriguing combination.

3 whole chicken breasts
6 slices prosciutto, page 6,
   (about 1/4 lb.)
6 slices Italian fontina cheese,
   (about 2 oz.), or
   6 tablespoons Parmesan cheese
3 fresh sage leaves
1 cup all-purpose flour

1 cup milk
3 tablespoons butter
1 tablespoon olive oil
1 chicken bouillon cube, crushed
1 cup dry white wine
Salt and freshly ground pepper to taste
1/3 cup whipping cream

Skin, bone and split chicken breasts, page 90. Put 1 slice prosciutto, 1 slice fontina cheese or 1 tablespoon Parmesan cheese, and half a sage leaf on each breast. Roll up chicken breasts and secure with wooden picks. Spread flour on aluminum foil. Dip chicken breasts in milk, then roll in flour to coat. Melt butter with oil in a large skillet. When butter foams, add chicken breasts. Cook over medium heat until golden on all sides. Add bouillon cube and 1/2 cup wine to chicken. Season with salt and pepper. When wine is reduced by half, add remaining wine. Cover skillet and reduce heat. Simmer 15 to 20 minutes or until chicken is tender. Turn chicken several times during cooking. Add a little more wine if sauce looks too dry. Place chicken on a warm platter. Increase heat and add cream. Deglaze skillet by stirring to dissolve meat juices attached to bottom of skillet. Taste and adjust sauce for seasoning, then spoon over chicken. Serve immediately. Makes 4 servings.

How to Make Stuffed Chicken Breasts

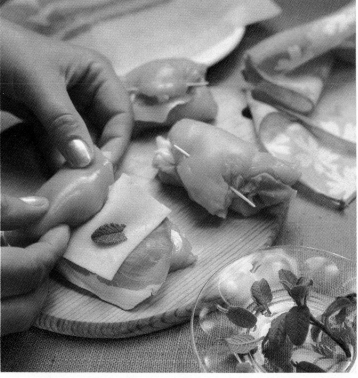

1/Roll up chicken breasts and secure with wooden picks.

2/When butter foams in skillet, add chicken breasts.

Chicken Breasts with Marsala Wine

Petti di Pollo al Marsala

Elegant yet economical, this dish is an all-time favorite.

4 whole chicken breasts
2 eggs
Salt and freshly ground pepper to taste
1-1/2 cups dry unflavored breadcrumbs

1/3 cup freshly grated Parmesan cheese
1/4 cup butter
2 tablespoons olive oil
1 cup dry Marsala wine or port

Remove skin from chicken breasts. Ease flesh away from bones with a sharp knife. Cut boned breasts in half. Beat eggs with salt and pepper in a medium bowl. Combine breadcrumbs and Parmesan cheese in a small bowl. Spread on aluminum foil. Dip chicken breasts in beaten eggs, then coat with breadcrumb mixture. Press mixture onto chicken with the palms of your hands. Let coated chicken stand 10 to 15 minutes. Melt butter with oil in a large heavy skillet. When butter foams, add chicken breasts. Cook over medium heat 2 to 3 minutes on each side or until chicken has a light-golden crust. Add Marsala or port. Cover skillet and reduce heat. Simmer 15 to 20 minutes or until chicken is tender. If sauce looks too dry, add a little more Marsala or port. Turn chicken several times during cooking. Place chicken on a warm platter. Taste and adjust sauce for seasoning, then spoon over chicken. Serve immediately. Makes 8 servings.

How to Bone Chicken Breasts

1/Ease chicken flesh away from bones with a sharp knife.

2/Cut boned breasts in half.

Chicken Hunter-Style

Pollo alla Cacciatora

This is the way we make this popular dish in Emilia-Romagna.

1 oz. dried wild Italian mushrooms or
   1/2 lb. fresh mushrooms, thinly sliced
1 cup warm water, if using dried mushrooms
2 tablespoons olive oil, if using
   fresh mushrooms
2 cups canned crushed Italian-style or
   whole tomatoes
1 (3- to 3-1/2-lb.) frying chicken,
   cut into serving pieces

1/2 cup all-purpose flour
3 to 4 tablespoons olive oil
2 garlic cloves
1 medium onion, thinly sliced
1/4 lb. pancetta, page 6,
   cut into 4 slices and diced
3/4 cup dry Marsala wine or dry white wine
Salt and freshly ground pepper to taste

If using dried mushrooms, soak in warm water 20 minutes. Drain mushrooms, reserving liquid. Strain mushroom liquid. Rinse mushrooms under cold running water. Squeeze to remove as much moisture as possible. If using fresh mushrooms, sauté in 2 tablespoons oil until golden; set aside. Press tomatoes through a food mill or sieve, page 161, to remove seeds. Wash and dry chicken pieces thoroughly. Spread flour on aluminum foil. Coat chicken pieces with flour. Heat 3 to 4 tablespoons oil in a large heavy casserole. Add garlic and chicken. Brown chicken on all sides over medium heat. Discard garlic. Remove chicken from casserole. Add onion to casserole and sauté until pale yellow. Add pancetta and sauté a few minutes longer. Return chicken to casserole. Increase heat and add Marsala or white wine. When wine is reduced by half, add tomato pulp. If using dried mushrooms, add to chicken mixture with reserved liquid. Cover casserole and reduce heat. Simmer 30 to 40 minutes or until chicken is tender. Turn and baste chicken a few times during cooking. If using sautéed fresh mushrooms, add to casserole during last 5 minutes of cooking. Season with salt and pepper. Serve hot. Makes 4 servings.

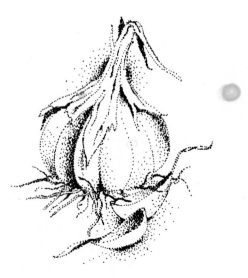

Most dishes cooked in sauce can be prepared ahead because the meat will stay moist. The flavors will blend and intensify.

Broiled Cornish Hens

Pollastrino alla Diavola

Cornish hens make perfect substitutes for the small, young chickens used in Italy.

4 Cornish hens
1/3 cup olive oil
Salt and freshly ground pepper to taste

Lemon wedges
Parsley

Cut Cornish hens lengthwise along entire backbone. Open out Cornish hens until flat. Place skin-side down on a cutting board. With a large cleaver or meat pounder, flatten cornish hens without breaking bones. Wash and dry thoroughly. Combine oil and salt and plenty of pepper in a small bowl. Brush Cornish hens on both sides with oil mixture. Place in a large shallow dish. Pour remaining oil over hens. Let stand 2 to 3 hours, basting several times with oil mixture. Preheat broiler or prepare barbecue. Arrange Cornish hens skin side facing heat. Cook 10 to 15 minutes. If skin turns too dark, adjust position of Cornish hens. Turn and baste with marinade. Cook 10 to 15 minutes longer or until tender. Season with additional pepper. Place on a warm platter. Garnish with lemon wedges and parsley. Serve immediately. Makes 4 servings.

Florentine Chicken

Pollo alla Fiorentina

A firm favorite for young and old alike.

1 (2- to 2-1/2-lb.) frying chicken
Salt and freshly ground pepper to taste
1 tablespoon chopped parsley
1/2 cup olive oil

Juice of 1 lemon
3/4 cup all-purpose flour
2 eggs
Oil for frying

Cut chicken into 14 to 16 small pieces or ask the butcher to do so. Wash and dry pieces thoroughly. Place chicken pieces in a large bowl. Season with salt and pepper and sprinkle with parsley. Add oil and lemon juice; mix well. Let stand 2 to 3 hours. Spread flour on aluminum foil. Beat eggs with salt and pepper in a medium bowl. Remove chicken from marinade and pat dry with paper towels. Coat chicken lightly with flour. Dip into beaten eggs; let excess egg drip off. Pour oil 2 inches deep in a large saucepan or deep-fryer. Heat oil to 375F (190C) or until a 1-inch cube of bread turns golden brown after 1 minute. Fry chicken pieces 10 to 12 minutes or until golden on all sides. Drain on paper towels. Place chicken pieces on a warm platter, sprinkle lightly with salt. Serve immediately. Makes 4 servings.

How to Make Broiled Cornish Hens

1/Cut Cornish hens lengthwise along backbone.

2/Serve on a warm platter, garnished with lemon and parsley.

Chicken with Mushrooms, Mustard & Lemon

Pollo all'Alba

Cooking chicken in canned chicken broth gives the meat excellent flavor.

6 cups canned chicken broth	1/2 lb. small white mushrooms
3 cups water	2 teaspoons mustard
2 carrots, chopped	Juice of 2 lemons
1 celery stalk, chopped	Salt and freshly ground pepper to taste
1 medium onion, sliced	4 flat anchovy fillets, chopped
3 whole chicken breasts	1/2 cup olive oil

Place broth, water, carrots, celery and onion in a large saucepan. Bring to a boil. Add chicken breasts. Cover saucepan and reduce heat. Simmer 40 to 50 minutes or until chicken is tender. Wash and dry mushrooms thoroughly and slice thin. Remove chicken from broth, reserving broth for other uses. Set chicken aside until cool. Bone and skin cooled chicken. Slice meat into thin strips. Place sliced chicken in a large salad bowl. Add sliced mushrooms. Combine mustard, lemon juice and salt and pepper in a small bowl. Add anchovies and oil; mix to blend. Taste and adjust anchovy dressing for seasoning, then pour over chicken mixture. Toss gently. Serve at room temperature. Makes 6 servings.

Turkey Breast Bologna-Style

Petto di Tacchino alla Bolognese

From Bologna a classic but simple dish.

2 lbs. turkey scaloppine
1/2 cup all-purpose flour
Salt and freshly ground pepper to taste
2 tablespoons tomato paste
1/2 cup water
3 tablespoons butter
2 tablespoons olive oil

1/2 cup dry Marsala wine or sherry
1/2 cup whipping cream
1/2 lb. prosciutto, page 6, or
  boiled ham, sliced
About 1/2 cup freshly grated
  Parmesan cheese

Place turkey scaloppine between 2 pieces of waxed paper and pound lightly. When pounding meat do not use a straight up-and-down movement. Use a sliding action so meat is stretched more than flattened. Place scaloppine on aluminum foil. Coat meat lightly with flour. Sprinkle with salt and pepper. Dilute tomato paste in 1/2 cup water. Melt butter with oil in a large heavy skillet. When butter foams, add turkey. Cook over high heat about 1 minute on each side or until lightly browned. Place turkey on a warm platter. Add Marsala or sherry to skillet. Deglaze by stirring to dissolve meat juices attached to bottom of skillet. Add cream and stir until bubbling. Stir diluted tomato paste into cream mixture. Place 1 slice prosciutto or boiled ham over each scaloppina and sprinkle with 1 tablespoon Parmesan cheese. Return to skillet. Cover and reduce heat. Simmer 3 to 5 minutes or until cheese is melted. Place scaloppine on a warm platter. Taste and adjust sauce for seasoning, then spoon over turkey. Serve immediately. Makes 6 servings.

Turkey Breast Bologna-Style; Roasted Potato Balls, page 140; Tomatoes with Piquant Green Sauce, page 133; and String Bean Salad with Oil & Lemon, page 148

Turkey Stuffed with Chestnuts

Tacchino Ripieno

You can find dried chestnuts in Italian specialty stores.

Chestnut Stuffing, see below
1 (10- to 12-lb.) turkey
Salt and freshly ground pepper to taste
1/4 cup butter, melted
Leaves from 1 sprig fresh rosemary or
  1 teaspoon dried rosemary

1 sprig fresh sage or
  1/2 teaspoon rubbed sage
About 3/4 cup dry white wine
1/3 cup Chicken Broth, page 20, or
  canned chicken broth, if desired

Chestnut Stuffing:
1/2 lb. dried chestnuts
1/2 lb. pitted prunes
1/4 lb. sweet Italian sausage
1/4 lb. pancetta, page 6,
  cut into 4 slices and diced

1 cup chopped walnuts
2 pears
2 apples
Salt to taste
1/3 cup brandy

Prepare Chestnut Stuffing. Preheat oven to 350F (175C). Butter a large roasting pan. Wash and dry turkey thoroughly. Season with salt and pepper inside bird and outside. Stuff cavity at neck end of turkey. Close tightly using thread or skewers. Place turkey breast-side up in buttered roasting pan. Brush turkey with melted butter. Sprinkle rosemary and sage over turkey. Roast 20 to 25 minutes per pound, 3 to 3-1/2 hours. Baste several times during cooking with turkey juices or 1/2 cup white wine. If turkey becomes too brown, cover with aluminum foil. Place on a large cutting board and cool 5 minutes. Carve turkey and arrange on a large warm platter. Keep warm in oven while preparing sauce. Remove as much fat as possible from pan juices. Place roasting pan over high heat. Add 1/3 cup white wine or chicken broth. Deglaze pan by stirring to dissolve juices attached to bottom of pan. Boil sauce until reduced to a medium-thick consistency. Strain and place in a sauce-boat. Serve turkey, stuffing and sauce hot. Makes 8 to 10 servings.

Chestnut Stuffing:
Place chestnuts in a large bowl. Add enough water to cover and soak overnight. Rinse chestnuts, removing any skin still attached. Place in a medium saucepan. Add enough water to cover. Bring water to a boil, then reduce heat to medium. Cook chestnuts 30 to 40 minutes or until tender. Drain and set aside. Place prunes in a large bowl. Add enough water to cover and soak 30 minutes. Remove skin from sausage and break into small pieces. Put sausage and pancetta in a medium skillet. Sauté over medium heat 5 to 10 minutes or until sausage loses its raw color. Place in a large bowl. Squeeze excess water from prunes. Chop prunes and chestnuts. Add to sausage mixture with walnuts. Peel and dice apples and pears. Add to sausage mixture. Season with salt and pepper. Stir in brandy. Taste and adjust for seasoning.

When you buy breadcrumbs, select those without herbs or seasonings. Otherwise the taste of your dish will be changed.

Turkey Croquettes

Crocchette di Tacchino

A marvelous way to transform leftover turkey into an inviting dish.

**Basic White Sauce, page 158, made with
   1 cup milk
3 to 4 cups chopped turkey
1/2 lb. mortadella or boiled ham,
   finely chopped
1 egg, lightly beaten**

**1/2 teaspoon freshly grated nutmeg
3/4 cup freshly grated Parmesan cheese
Salt and freshly ground pepper to taste
1-1/2 to 2 cups dry unflavored breadcrumbs
Oil for frying**

Prepare Basic White Sauce; let cool to room temperature. Place turkey and mortadella or boiled ham in a large bowl. Add egg, nutmeg, 1/2 cup Parmesan cheese, white sauce and salt and pepper. Mix thoroughly. Combine 1/4 cup Parmesan cheese and breadcrumbs in a small bowl. Spread on aluminum foil. Take a generous tablespoon of turkey mixture and form a small sausage. Roll in breadcrumb mixture to coat. Press crumbs lightly onto croquette. Repeat until all mixture is used. Pour oil 1 inch deep in a large skillet or saucepan. Heat oil until a 1-inch cube of bread turns golden brown almost immediately. Using a slotted spoon, lower a few croquettes at a time into hot oil. Turn croquettes. When golden on all sides, remove from oil with slotted spoon. Drain on paper towels. Arrange croquettes on a warm platter. Serve immediately. Makes 6 servings.

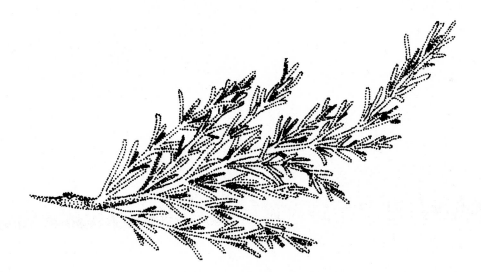

Lamb

Lamb in Italy is synonymous with Easter and spring because these are the times it is traditionally served. Italians like to eat lamb when it is three to four months old. At that age, lamb has a tender, delicate flavor and its meat is light pink.

In many other countries, lamb goes to market a little older, at seven to eight months. It is still good at that age with a darker and well-marbled meat. As lamb gets older it becomes mutton. A whole leg of lamb should weigh four to six pounds. If it exceeds nine pounds, you are probably buying mutton.

Lamb can provide some extremely elegant dishes. Rack of lamb roasted with a tasty breadcrumb coating is a treat for eye and palate. Lamb chops dipped in eggs, then coated with a Parmesan cheese and breadcrumb mixture, are unbelievably succulent. A whole leg of lamb braised in a tomato-based mixture prompted one of my students to claim that although he was born and raised on a ranch and had eaten lamb all his life, this was the best he had ever tasted.

Menu

Prosciutto with Melon, page 13
Baked Semolina Gnocchi, page 61
Leg of Lamb with Bacon
& Vegetables, page 100
Mixed Salad, page 149
Fresh Fruit
Gattinara or *Pinot Noir

*California wine

Pork & Variety Meats

Some less expensive cuts of lamb can give you equally delicious dishes. For skewered lamb, either the leg or the shoulder can be used. For stewed lamb, the shoulder is your best bet.

Italians eat a considerable amount of pork, mostly in the form of sausage and ham. There are many dishes in northern Italian cuisine in which pork is barely visible but is vital to flavor. Pancetta, for example, plays a subtle but important role in cooking. Prosciutto, a sweet and delicate unsmoked ham, is eaten alone or as a topping or stuffing for roasts or chops.

In Italy, we have stores called *salumerie*. These are pork butcher shops, almost delicatessens, where all pork products are sold. These are the showcases for an unbelievable array of sausages, salami and prosciutti among other items. Most of these products are preserved, salt and air cured, then aged to perfection. Some are fresh like the famous *cotechino*. Cotechino is a large fresh sausage, a specialty of Emilia-Romagna. It is made from pork rind and shoulder, salt, pepper and nutmeg. Try fresh sausages, fried or braised and served with hot *polenta*, for an unbeatable combination.

Pork chops and pork roasts are a favorite of many regions. A beautiful pork-loin roast cooked with a little Marsala wine becomes a delicious and elegant glazed dish. Braise a pork loin in milk and you will have a melt-in-your-mouth delicacy. Roast pork with a little fresh rosemary and garlic and discover an unbeatable combination.

Many Italians enjoy variety meats such as sweetbreads, brains and liver. When you cook Calf's Liver in Onion Sauce, you will taste one of northern Italy's most celebrated liver dishes.

I learned to like calf's liver as a young child. My mother would say, "Tonight we'll have breaded chicken." Only when I was older did I realize that the strange-looking chicken was liver. By then it was too late because I had grown to like it.

Both liver recipes in this chapter can be cooked in a few minutes. This is one more advantage of the food of Italy. It is outstanding and yet so simple to prepare.

Roast Rack of Lamb

Carré d'Agnello Arrosto

Serve with Baked Onions, page 136, and fresh vegetables in season.

2 racks of lamb	2 tablespoons chopped parsley
2 tablespoons olive oil	3 garlic cloves, chopped
Leaves from 1 sprig fresh rosemary or	1 tablespoon dry unflavored breadcrumbs
1 teaspoon dried rosemary	1 tablespoon freshly grated Parmesan cheese
Salt and freshly ground pepper to taste	

Trim all fat from lamb. Preheat oven to 375F (190C). Brush lamb with 1 tablespoon oil and sprinkle with rosemary. Season with salt and pepper. Put 1 tablespoon oil in a roasting pan. Place lamb in pan. Bake 30 to 35 minutes to give medium-rare meat. Bake another 5 minutes for medium to well-done meat. Combine parsley, garlic, breadcrumbs and Parmesan cheese in a small bowl. Sprinkle top of lamb with breadcrumb mixture and cook 5 minutes longer. Place meat on a warm platter. Serve individual chops by cutting down between the ribs. Makes 4 to 6 servings.

Leg of Lamb with Bacon & Vegetables

Cosciotto d'Agnello alla Pancetta

A good way to make a leg of lamb feed a crowd.

3 to 4 tablespoons olive oil
1 (4- to 5-lb.) leg of lamb
Salt and freshly ground pepper to taste
1/4 lb. pancetta, page 6,
   cut into 4 slices and diced
1 medium onion, sliced
2 carrots, finely chopped

1 celery stalk, finely chopped
1 cup dry white wine
1 (28-oz.) can crushed Italian-style or
   whole tomatoes
3 tablespoons chopped parsley
2 garlic cloves, chopped
Water, if needed

Heat oil in a large heavy casserole. Season lamb with salt and pepper and place in casserole. Brown lamb on all sides over medium heat. Remove lamb from casserole. Add pancetta, onion, carrots and celery to casserole. Sauté until lightly browned. Return lamb to casserole. Increase heat and add wine. Cook until wine is reduced by half. Stir in tomatoes and cover casserole. Cook over medium-low heat 2 to 2-1/2 hours or until tender. Stir sauce frequently and use to baste lamb. Add parsley and garlic during last 5 minutes of cooking. If sauce becomes too thick, add a little water. Place lamb on a cutting board and cool 5 minutes. Keep sauce warm. Slice lamb and arrange on a warm platter. Taste and adjust sauce for seasoning, then spoon over meat. Serve immediately. Makes 6 to 8 servings.

Fried Lamb Chops

Costolette di Agnello Fritte

Use very young lamb for a succulent and delicate dish.

8 single-rib lamb chops
2 eggs
Salt and freshly ground pepper to taste
1/2 cup all-purpose flour

3/4 cup freshly grated Parmesan cheese
3/4 cup dry unflavored breadcrumbs
1/4 cup butter
2 tablespoons olive oil

Trim all fat from lamb chops. Beat eggs with salt and pepper in a medium bowl. Spread flour on aluminum foil. Combine Parmesan cheese and breadcrumbs in a small bowl. Spread on a second piece of foil. Coat chops lightly with flour. Dip chops in beaten eggs, then coat with breadcrumb mixture. Press mixture onto chops with the palms of your hands. Let coated chops stand 10 to 15 minutes. Melt butter with oil in a large skillet. When butter foams, add chops. Cook over medium heat 2 to 3 minutes on each side or until meat has a light-golden crust. Drain chops on paper towels. Place chops on a warm platter. Season with salt. Serve immediately. Makes 4 servings.

Leg of Lamb with Bacon & Vegetables

Skewered Lamb

Agnellino allo Spiedo

In Italy, tender young lamb is cooked on an open spit. Broiling also gives excellent results.

1 (3- to 3-1/2-lb.) leg of lamb	1/4 cup olive oil
Marinade, see below	2 medium onions, cut into large pieces
1/2 lb. pancetta, page 6,	3 tomatoes, quartered
cut into 4 slices	Additional olive oil
1/3 cup chopped parsley	Salt and freshly ground pepper to taste
4 garlic cloves, chopped	

Marinade:

4 to 5 cups dry white wine	3 garlic cloves, crushed
2 sprigs fresh rosemary or	4 to 5 fresh bay leaves or
2 teaspoons dried rosemary	1 teaspoon crushed dried bay leaves
5 fresh sage leaves or	1 medium onion, sliced
1 teaspoon rubbed sage	Salt and freshly ground pepper to taste

Trim all fat from lamb and cut in 2- to 2-1/2-inch cubes. Prepare Marinade. Combine meat and marinade in a large bowl; stir well. Cover and refrigerate overnight. Preheat broiler or prepare barbecue. Cut pancetta into large pieces. Mix parsley, garlic and 1/4 cup oil in a small bowl. Set aside. Drain lamb and dry on paper towels. Alternate lamb on skewers with pancetta, onion pieces and tomato quarters. Brush with oil. Broil to preferred doneness, brushing frequently with oil during cooking. A few minutes before removing meat from broiler, brush lamb with parsley-garlic mixture. Season with salt and pepper. Serve immediately. Makes 8 servings.

Marinade:
Combine ingredients in a medium bowl.

How to Make Skewered Lamb

1/Cut pancetta into large pieces.

2/Alternate lamb on skewers with pancetta, onion and tomato.

Lamb Stew Bologna-Style

Spezzatino di Agnello alla Bolognese

A loaf of bread and a bottle of red wine will add the perfect touch to this simple meal.

1 (2- to 2-1/2-lb.) boneless shoulder of lamb	2 garlic cloves, chopped

1-1/2 cups canned crushed Italian-style or
  whole tomatoes
	2 or 3 sprigs fresh rosemary or
	   1 tablespoon dried rosemary

3 tablespoons olive oil	3/4 cup light, red wine
3 tablespoons butter	Salt and freshly ground pepper to taste

Trim all fat from lamb. Cut meat in 1-1/2- to 2-inch cubes. Press tomatoes through a food mill or sieve, page 161, to remove seeds. Heat oil in a medium skillet. Add lamb. Sauté over medium heat 2 to 3 minutes or until lamb is colored on all sides. Remove lamb from skillet. Discard all fat from skillet. Add butter to skillet. When butter foams, add garlic and rosemary. Return lamb to skillet. Before garlic changes color, stir in wine. When wine is reduced by half, add tomato pulp. Season with salt and pepper. Cook uncovered 25 to 30 minutes over medium heat, stirring occasionally. Serve hot. Makes 4 to 6 servings.

Pork Loin with Garlic & Rosemary

Arista alla Fiorentina

A very old Florentine dish that goes back as far as the fifteenth century.

6 garlic cloves, finely chopped
Leaves from 6 sprigs fresh rosemary or
   2 tablespoons dried rosemary

Salt and freshly ground pepper to taste
1 (3- to 3-1/2-lb.) boneless pork-loin roast
2 or 3 tablespoons olive oil

Preheat oven to 375F (190C). Combine garlic, rosemary and salt and pepper in a small bowl. With a thin knife, make 7 to 8 slits about 1/2 inch deep in meat. Fill slits with half the garlic-rosemary mixture. Spread remaining mixture over meat. Put oil in a roasting pan. Place meat in pan and insert a meat thermometer. Bake 2 to 2-1/2 hours or until meat reaches preferred doneness according to meat thermometer. Baste meat frequently with its own juices. Place meat on a cutting board and cool 5 minutes. Slice meat and arrange on a warm platter. Serve immediately with a few tablespoons of its own juices. Makes 6 to 8 servings.

Pork Loin Braised in Milk

Arrosto di Maiale al Latte

Tender, juicy and delicate, this old Bolognese dish is a winner.

2 tablespoons butter
2 tablespoons olive oil
1 (3- to 3-1/2-lb.) boneless pork-loin roast
Salt and freshly ground pepper to taste

2-1/2 cups milk
1/2 cup whipping cream
2 tablespoons freshly grated Parmesan cheese

Melt butter with oil in a large heavy casserole. When butter foams, add pork. Brown pork on all sides over medium heat. Season with salt and pepper. Stir in milk and bring to a boil. Partially cover casserole and reduce heat. Cook meat 2 to 2-1/2 hours or until tender. Baste meat several times during cooking. If sauce looks too dry during cooking, add a little more milk. Place meat on a cutting board. By the end of cooking time, only 1 or 2 tablespoons of thick milky sauce should be left in casserole. If too much sauce remains, cook uncovered over high heat 10 to 15 minutes. Remove as much fat as possible from sauce. Add cream and Parmesan cheese to sauce. Stir with a wooden spoon over high heat to dissolve meat juices. Put sauce in a blender or food processor and process until smooth. Return sauce to casserole and simmer 1 to 2 minutes until sauce has a thick creamy consistency. Taste and adjust for seasoning. Slice meat and arrange on a large warm platter. Spoon sauce over meat. Serve immediately. Makes 6 to 8 servings.

Variation

Omit cream and Parmesan cheese. Cook pork uncovered during final 10 to 15 minutes over medium-high heat. Cook until all milk has evaporated and only brown particles remain in casserole.

Pork Loin with Marsala Wine

Arrosto di Maiale al Marsala

Add exciting color with Baked Tomatoes, page 133, and a green-vegetable salad.

1 (2-1/2- to 3-lb.) boneless pork-loin roast
Leaves from 3 sprigs fresh rosemary or
   1 tablespoon dried rosemary
2 garlic cloves, chopped
3 tablespoons butter

2 tablespoons olive oil
Salt and freshly ground pepper to taste
1 cup dry white wine
1/2 cup dry Marsala wine or sherry
1/3 cup whipping cream

Rub pork with rosemary and garlic. Melt butter with oil in a large heavy casserole. When butter foams, add pork. Brown meat on all sides over medium heat. Add salt and pepper. Add 3/4 cup white wine. Deglaze casserole by stirring to dissolve meat juices attached to bottom of casserole. Partially cover casserole and reduce heat. Cook meat 2 hours or until tender. Baste meat several times during cooking. If sauce looks too dry, add remaining wine. Place meat on a cutting board. Remove as much fat as possible from pan juices. Add Marsala or sherry and cream to pan juices. Stir over high heat until sauce has a medium-thick consistency. Taste and adjust for seasoning. Slice meat and arrange on a warm platter. Spoon sauce over meat. Serve immediately. Makes 6 servings.

Little Pork Bundles

Involtini Scappati

A tasty dish for family or company.

8 slices pork tenderloin,
   cut 3/8 inch thick
1/4 lb. pancetta, page 6,
   cut into 8 slices
3 tablespoons butter

1 tablespoon olive oil
2 or 3 fresh or dried bay leaves
Salt and freshly ground pepper to taste
1 cup dry white wine

Remove excess fat from pork loin. Place slices between 2 pieces of waxed paper and pound until thin. When pounding meat do not use a straight up and down movement. Use a sliding action so meat is stretched more than flattened. Place 1 slice pancetta over each slice of pork. Roll up pork and secure each roll with 1 or 2 wooden picks. Melt butter with oil in a medium skillet. When butter foams, add meat and bay leaves. Cook meat over medium heat until golden brown on all sides. Season with salt and pepper. Add wine. Cook uncovered 10 to 12 minutes or until wine is almost all evaporated. Only 1 or 2 tablespoons of thickened wine sauce should remain in skillet. Place meat on a warm platter. Spoon sauce over meat. Serve immediately. Makes 4 servings.

Variation

Substitute veal scaloppine for the pork.

Stuffed Pork Chops

Costolette di Maiale con Prosciutto

A rich, satisfying dish that will have your family and friends asking for more.

4 pork chops, 1 inch thick	**Salt and freshly ground pepper to taste**
2 oz. Italian fontina cheese or	**1 cup dry unflavored breadcrumbs**
** 4 tablespoons freshly grated**	**3 tablespoons butter**
** Parmesan cheese**	**2 tablespoons olive oil**
4 slices prosciutto, page 6, (about 2 oz.)	**1/2 cup dry Marsala wine or sherry**
2 eggs	

Make a pocket in each chop by cutting a horizontal slit as far as the bone. Cut fontina cheese into small pieces. Fill each chop with 1 slice prosciutto and a few pieces of fontina cheese or 1 tablespoon Parmesan cheese. Secure each chop with 2 wooden picks. Beat eggs with salt and pepper in a medium bowl. Spread breadcrumbs on aluminum foil. Dip chops in beaten eggs, then coat with breadcrumbs. Press breadcrumbs onto chops with the palms of your hands. Let coated chops stand 10 to 15 minutes. Melt butter with oil in a large skillet. When butter foams, add chops. Cook over medium heat 3 to 5 minutes on each side or until meat has a golden-brown crust. Add Marsala or sherry to skillet and stir well. Cover skillet and reduce heat. Simmer 20 to 25 minutes or until chops are tender. If sauce looks too dry, add a little more wine or water. Place chops on a warm platter. Spoon sauce over chops. Serve immediately. Makes 4 servings.

Pork Chops in Wine

Costolette di Maiale al Vino

Pork chops cooked this way are tender and flavorful.

2 eggs	**3 tablespoons butter**
Salt and freshly ground pepper to taste	**1 tablespoon olive oil**
1 cup dry unflavored breadcrumbs	**1 cup dry white wine**
4 pork chops, 3/4 inch thick	

Beat eggs with salt and pepper in a medium bowl. Spread breadcrumbs on aluminum foil. Dip chops in beaten eggs, then coat with breadcrumbs. Press breadcrumbs onto chops with the palms of your hands. Let coated chops stand 10 to 15 minutes. Melt butter with oil in a medium skillet. When butter foams, add chops. Cook over medium heat 3 to 5 minutes on each side or until meat has a golden-brown crust. Stir in wine. Cover skillet and reduce heat. Simmer 15 to 20 minutes or until wine is almost all evaporated and chops are tender. Add a little more wine if sauce is too dry. If too much wine remains after 15 minutes, uncover casserole for last 5 minutes of cooking. Place chops on a warm platter. Spoon sauce over chops. Serve immediately. Makes 4 servings.

How to Make Stuffed Pork Chops

1/Cut a horizontal slit as far as the bone in each chop.

2/Secure stuffed chops with wooden picks.

Pork Chops in Onion Sauce

Costolette di Maiale alla Cipolla

Onions become melt-in-your-mouth tender in this creamy sauce.

3 tablespoons butter
5 medium onions, thinly sliced
1/2 cup whipping cream
1 teaspoon sugar

1/2 cup all-purpose flour
4 pork chops, 3/4 inch thick
3 tablespoons olive oil
Salt and freshly ground pepper to taste

Melt butter in a large skillet. When butter foams, add onions. Cover skillet and cook over medium heat until onions are pale yellow. Stir in cream and sugar. Cook 2 minutes longer. Spread flour on aluminum foil. Coat chops with flour. Heat oil in a smaller skillet. Add chops and cook over medium heat 3 to 5 minutes on each side or until golden brown. Add chops to onion-cream mixture. Cover skillet and reduce heat. Simmer 15 to 20 minutes or until chops are tender. Season with salt and pepper. Place chops on a warm platter. Spoon sauce over chops. Serve immediately. Makes 4 servings.

Sausage with Friggione

Salsiccia con Friggione

Ideal for a carefree Sunday lunch with friends.

Friggione, page 129   **1 to 2 cups water**
1-1/2 to 2 lbs. sweet Italian sausages

Prepare Friggione. Wash sausages. Puncture sausages in several places with a fork. Put sausages and water in a large skillet. Bring water to a boil. Cook 10 to 15 minutes over medium heat, turning sausages during cooking. By the end of cooking time water should have evaporated leaving sausages and some of their fat in skillet. Brown sausages on all sides. Add Friggione to skillet. Cook Friggione and sausages 5 to 8 minutes longer. Serve immediately. Makes 4 to 6 servings.

Sausage & Beans in Tomato Sauce

Salsicce e Fagioli in Umido

This dish brings back memories of cold winter nights when simple food brought my family closer together.

1-1/2 cups dried white kidney beans or   **1 to 2 cups water**
   other white beans   **Salt and freshly ground pepper to taste**
2 cups Plain Tomato Sauce, page 161   **2 tablespoons chopped parsley**
1-1/2 lbs. sweet Italian sausages   **2 garlic cloves, chopped**

Place beans in a large bowl. Add enough cold water to cover beans. Soak overnight. Prepare Plain Tomato Sauce. Rinse beans under cold running water. Place beans in a large saucepan. Add enough salted water to cover. Bring water to a boil. Reduce heat. Cover pan and simmer beans until tender but firm, 40 to 50 minutes. Wash sausages. Puncture sausages in several places with a fork. Put 1 to 2 cups water and sausages in a large skillet. Bring water to a boil. Cook 10 to 15 minutes over medium heat, turning sausages during cooking. By the end of cooking time water should have evaporated leaving sausages and some of their fat in skillet. Add Plain Tomato Sauce to skillet. Season with salt and pepper. Add cooked beans. Simmer uncovered 5 minutes. Stir in parsley and garlic. Cook 5 minutes longer. Serve immediately. Makes 4 to 6 servings.

Boiled Cotechino Sausage

Cotechino Bollito

This large pork sausage is a specialty of the Emilia-Romagna region.

1 (2- to 2-1/2-lb.) cotechino sausage

Place sausage in a large bowl. Cover with cold water and soak overnight. Puncture sausage skin in several places with a fork. Place in a large saucepan. Cover with water. Bring water to a boil. Reduce heat and cover pan. Simmer sausage 1-1/2 to 2 hours, depending on size. When ready to serve, remove sausage from liquid. Remove and discard skin. Cut sausage into slices. Serve hot with mashed potatoes. Makes 4 to 6 servings.

Fried Calf's Liver

Fegato Fritto

Mistaking it for chicken as a child, I have grown to love liver cooked this way.

1 lb. calf's liver	Salt and freshly ground pepper to taste
1 cup very fine, dry unflavored breadcrumbs	Lemon wedges
5 tablespoons butter	
2 fresh sage leaves or	
1/2 teaspoon rubbed sage	

Cut liver into thin slices. Remove membrane and veins. Spread breadcrumbs on aluminum foil. Coat liver slices with breadcrumbs. Press breadcrumbs onto liver with the palms of your hands. Shake off excess breadcrumbs. Melt butter in a large skillet. When butter foams, add sliced liver and sage. Cook over medium heat 2 to 2-1/2 minutes on each side or until liver has a light-golden crust. Drain on paper towels. Season with salt and pepper. Place liver on a warm platter. Garnish with lemon wedges. Serve immediately. Makes 4 servings.

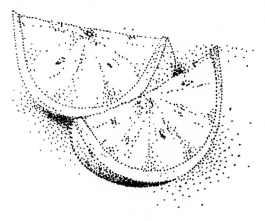

Calf's Liver in Onion Sauce

Piccata di Fegato alla Cipolla Fondente

A creation of a remarkable Milanese restaurateur, Gualtiero Marchesi.

1-1/2 lbs. onions	Chicken Broth, page 20, or
1-1/2 lbs. calf's liver	canned chicken broth, or water,
6 tablespoons butter	if needed
2 cups dry white wine	Fresh chervil or parsley
Salt and freshly ground pepper to taste	

Cut onions into very thin slices. Cut calf's liver into very thin slices. Remove membrane and veins. Combine 3 tablespoons butter, wine and sliced onions in a medium-size saucepan or casserole. Cook covered over low heat 30 minutes. Season with salt and pepper. Onions should be moist and creamy. If sauce looks too dry, add a little chicken broth or water. If there is too much liquid, increase heat and cook uncovered 3 to 5 minutes. Melt remaining butter in a large heavy skillet. When butter begins to turn brown, add sliced liver. Cook over high heat, 1-1/2 to 2 minutes on each side. Inside of liver should be pale pink. Spoon onion sauce onto 4 warm serving plates. Arrange 2 or 3 slices of liver on top of sauce. Garnish each serving with chervil or parsley. Serve immediately. Makes 4 servings.

Veal &

In Italy, milk-fed veal is one of the most popular meats.

Before we moved to California from New York, my husband was offered an attractive position in a renowned midwestern hospital. We took a trip there to explore his future job and the lifestyle. The state was very beautiful and the position offered to my husband was prestigious. Unfortunately, it was almost impossible to find Italian ingredients in the area. Milk-fed veal was rarely available. My husband turned down the job. We were ready to change our lifestyle, but not to the point of changing our eating habits so drastically. Today, it is easier to find Italian ingredients and milk-fed veal there.

Veal can be sautéed, braised, fried, stewed, roasted or poached. A popular example of a braised dish is Veal Shanks Milan-Style. Veal shanks are a relatively inexpensive cut of meat. When cooked by slow braising, the meat becomes tender enough to cut with a fork. If you intend to stew veal, use a less expensive cut. This usually comes from the shoulder. An excellent veal roast

Menu

*California wine

can be obtained from boned breast of veal. This is one of the less-expensive cuts. The veal can be stuffed and rolled, then pan-roasted. The result is a juicy, tender roast. Veal can be poached to produce one of the best and most famous northern Italian dishes, *Vitello Tonnato,* Cold Veal with Tuna Fish Sauce.

There are probably several reasons why beef is not a favorite with Italians. Whether these reasons stem from an innate preference or are the result of centuries of economic and social conditions, the fact remains. Yet, strangely enough, Italy produces some of the best beef in the world. A prize-winning beef, admired by cattle-raisers the world over, is the Chianina beef of Tuscany. The best charcoal-broiled steak of Italy is found in Florence and is made from Chianina beef.

Aside from the celebrated Florentine Steak, beef in Italy is used mostly in pot-roasts or stews cooked slowly with wine, herbs and vegetables.

In selecting beef, look for a rich color with marbling of fat. Marbling is important for a cut of meat that will be broiled or roasted. This cut of beef is generally more expensive but will be tender and juicy when cooked. A less-expensive cut of meat with less marbling is best for braising or stewing. The slow, moist cooking will produce tender and flavorful dishes.

When serving meat that will follow a pasta dish, try to balance and complement the two. If a rich, substantial first course like *lasagne* is served, the meat that follows should be extremely light and simple. Roast veal or pork, or veal scaloppine would be suitable. Even the vegetables should be served with a minimum of sauce. When a simple first course like Risotto with Parmesan Cheese, page 70, is served, the meat that follows can have a variety of sauces. Choose Braised Beef in Barolo Wine or Eggplants & Cutlets Parmigiana.

I hope one point will be clear from this chapter and throughout the book. A grasp of the underlying mood of northern Italian cuisine is more important than a technically perfect execution of a recipe.

Veal Chops Milan-Style

Costolette di Vitello alla Milanese

Who said it takes forever to cook good Italian food? This dish proves otherwise.

6 veal loin chops, 3/4 inch thick
3/4 cup dry unflavored breadcrumbs
1/3 cup freshly grated Parmesan cheese
2 eggs

Salt to taste
1/4 cup butter
Lemon slices

Pound veal chops lightly. Combine breadcrumbs and Parmesan cheese in a small bowl. Spread on aluminum foil. Beat eggs with salt in a medium bowl. Dip chops in beaten eggs, then coat with breadcrumb mixture. Press mixture onto chops with the palms of your hands. Let coated chops stand 10 to 15 minutes. Melt butter in a large skillet. When butter foams, add chops. Cook over medium heat 4 to 5 minutes on each side or until meat has a golden-brown crust. Drain on paper towels. Place chops on a warm platter. Garnish with lemon slices. Serve immediately. Makes 6 servings.

Veal Scaloppine with Marsala Wine

Scaloppine di Vitello al Marsala

Veal scaloppine should be cooked and served immediately. Reheating will toughen and dry the meat.

2 lbs. veal scaloppine
1/2 cup all-purpose flour
Salt and freshly ground pepper to taste

1/4 cup butter
1 tablespoon olive oil
3/4 cup dry Marsala wine or sherry

Place scaloppine between 2 pieces of waxed paper and pound until thin. When pounding meat do not use a straight up-and-down movement. Use a sliding action so meat is stretched more than flattened. Place scaloppine on aluminum foil. Coat meat lightly with flour. Sprinkle with salt and pepper. Melt 3 tablespoons butter with oil in a large heavy skillet. When butter foams, add veal. Cook over high heat about 1 minute on each side. Veal should be light golden outside and pink inside. Remove veal from skillet. Add 1 tablespoon butter and Marsala or sherry. Deglaze skillet by stirring to dissolve meat juices attached to bottom of skillet. When wine is reduced by half, return veal to skillet. Mix gently with sauce. Place meat on a warm platter. Spoon sauce over meat. Serve immediately. Makes 6 to 8 servings.

Veal Scaloppine in Lemon Sauce

Scaloppine di Vitello all'Agro

This dish should be made at the last moment and brought to the table quickly.

1-1/2 to 2 lbs. veal scaloppine
1/2 cup all-purpose flour
Salt and freshly ground pepper to taste
1/4 cup butter
1 tablespoon olive oil

Juice of 1 lemon
3 tablespoons chopped parsley
2 garlic cloves, chopped
2 tablespoons capers

Place scaloppine between 2 pieces of waxed paper and pound until thin. When pounding meat do not use a straight up-and-down movement. Use a sliding action so meat is stretched more than flattened. Place scaloppine on aluminum foil. Coat meat lightly with flour. Sprinkle with salt and pepper. Melt 3 tablespoons butter with oil in a large heavy skillet. When butter foams, add veal. Cook over high heat about 1 minute on each side. Veal should be light golden outside and pink inside. Place veal on a warm platter. Add 1 tablespoon butter and lemon juice to skillet. Deglaze skillet by stirring to dissolve meat juices attached to bottom of skillet. Stir in parsley, garlic and capers. Taste and adjust sauce for seasoning, then spoon over veal. Serve immediately. Makes 4 to 6 servings.

Tidbits of Veal in Cream Sauce

Bocconcini di Vitello alla Crema

Veal cooked in cream or milk acquires a light, creamy texture.

**1/2 cup Chicken Broth, page 20, or
   canned chicken broth**
2-1/2 lbs. shoulder of veal
1/2 cup all-purpose flour
1/4 cup butter
1 large onion, chopped

1/2 cup dry white wine
Salt and white pepper to taste
1/2 cup whipping cream
Juice of 1 lemon
2 egg yolks, lightly beaten

Prepare Chicken Broth. Cut veal into 1-1/2- to 2-inch cubes. Place on aluminum foil and sprinkle with flour. Melt butter in a large heavy casserole. When butter foams, add onion. Sauté over medium-low heat until pale yellow. Add veal to casserole. Brown on all sides over medium heat. Increase heat and stir in wine. When wine is reduced by half, season with salt and pepper. Add chicken broth. Cover casserole and reduce heat. Simmer 35 to 40 minutes or until meat is tender. Stir occasionally during cooking. Stir in cream. Cook uncovered 10 minutes longer. Place veal on a warm platter. Put sauce and lemon juice in a blender or food processor and process until smooth. Return sauce to casserole. Gradually add egg yolks, stirring constantly until sauce is thick and creamy. Taste and adjust sauce for seasoning, then spoon over veal. Serve immediately. Makes 6 servings.

Winter-Style Veal Stew

Bocconcini di Vitello all'Invernale

This marvelous stew tastes even better if prepared one or two days ahead.

2-1/2 lbs. shoulder of veal
1/2 cup all-purpose flour
2 tablespoons butter
2 tablespoons olive oil
1 medium onion, finely chopped
1 carrot, finely chopped

1 celery stalk, finely chopped
1/2 cup dry white wine
**1 (16-oz.) can crushed Italian-style or
   whole tomatoes**
Salt and freshly ground pepper to taste
1 (10-oz.) pkg. frozen small peas, thawed

Cut veal into 1-1/2- to 2-inch cubes. Place on aluminum foil and sprinkle with flour. Melt butter with oil in a large heavy casserole. When butter foams, add veal and brown on all sides over medium heat. Add onion, carrot and celery. Sauté until lightly browned. Stir in wine. When wine is reduced by half, add tomatoes. Season with salt and pepper. Cover casserole and reduce heat. Simmer 40 to 45 minutes or until meat is tender and sauce has a medium-thick consistency. If sauce is too thin, increase heat and cook uncovered about 10 minutes. Add peas and cook 5 minutes longer. Serve hot. Makes 6 to 8 servings.

Veal Shanks Milan-Style

Ossobuco alla Milanese

The perfect accompaniment for this dish is Risotto Milan-Style, page 69.

6 veal shanks, 2 inches thick
1/2 cup all-purpose flour
1/3 cup olive oil
1 medium onion, finely chopped
1 carrot, finely chopped
1 celery stalk, finely chopped
3/4 cup dry white wine

1 (28-oz.) can crushed
   Italian-style tomatoes
2 tablespoons chopped parsley
2 garlic cloves, finely chopped
Salt and freshly ground pepper to taste
Additional chopped parsley

Place veal shanks on aluminum foil and sprinkle with flour. Heat oil in a large heavy casserole. Add veal to casserole. Brown on all sides over medium heat. Remove meat from casserole. Add onion, carrot and celery. Sauté until lightly browned. Return veal to casserole. Stir in wine. When wine is reduced by half, add tomatoes. Cover casserole and reduce heat. Simmer 1-1/2 hours or until meat falls away from the bone. Add 2 tablespoons parsley and garlic. Season with salt and pepper. Arrange meat and sauce on a warm platter. Garnish with additional parsley. Serve immediately. Makes 6 servings.

Variation

Brown veal in butter. Substitute 1-1/2 cups Meat Broth, page 19, for the tomatoes.

How to Make Veal Shanks Milan-Style

1/Add tomatoes to casserole when wine is reduced by half.

2/Arrange meat and sauce on a warm platter. Garnish with parsley.

Veal Shanks Trieste-Style

Ossobuco alla Triestina

When properly cooked, the meat should be tender enough to cut with a fork.

1 cup Chicken Broth, page 20, or
   canned chicken broth
3 tablespoons butter
2 tablespoons olive oil
3 large onions, thinly sliced
6 veal shanks, 2 inches thick
1 cup all-purpose flour

Salt and freshly ground pepper to taste
1 cup dry white wine
3 tablespoons chopped parsley
2 garlic cloves, chopped
3 flat anchovy fillets, mashed
Grated zest of 2 lemons

Prepare Chicken Broth. Melt butter with oil in a large heavy casserole. When butter foams, add onions. Sauté over medium heat until pale yellow. Remove onions from casserole. Place veal shanks on aluminum foil and sprinkle with flour. Add veal to casserole. Brown on all sides over medium heat. Season with salt and pepper. Return onions to casserole. Add wine. When wine is reduced by half, add chicken broth. Cover casserole and reduce heat. Simmer 1-1/2 hours or until meat falls away from the bone. Stir in parsley, garlic, anchovies and lemon zest. If sauce is too thin, remove meat and boil sauce uncovered about 10 minutes. If sauce is too thick, add a little more chicken broth. Taste and adjust for seasoning. Arrange meat and sauce on a warm platter. Serve immediately. Makes 6 servings.

Roast Breast of Veal with Vegetables

Petto di Vitello al Forno con Verdure

Breast of veal is surprisingly economical and very tasty.

1-1/2 cups canned crushed Italian-style or
   whole tomatoes
3 tablespoons butter
2 tablespoons olive oil
1 (3- to 3-1/2-lb.) boneless breast of
   veal roast
1 medium onion, finely chopped
1 carrot, finely chopped
1 celery stalk, finely chopped
1 potato, peeled, finely chopped

2 garlic cloves
2 dried bay leaves
1/2 teaspoon whole black peppercorns
1/4 lb. pancetta, page 6,
   cut into 4 slices and diced
3/4 cup dry white wine
1 teaspoon sugar
Salt and freshly ground pepper to taste
1 chicken bouillon cube, crushed
Water, if needed

Preheat oven to 375F (190C). Press tomatoes through a food mill or sieve, page 161, to remove seeds. Melt butter with oil in a large heavy casserole. When butter foams, add veal. Brown on all sides over medium heat. Add onion, carrot, celery, potato, garlic, bay leaves, peppercorns and pancetta. Sauté until vegetables and pancetta are lightly browned. Stir in wine. Add sugar and season with salt and pepper. Cook until wine is reduced by half. Add crushed bouillon cube and tomato pulp. Bring to a boil. Cover casserole and place in oven. Cook 1-1/2 to 2 hours or until meat is tender. Baste meat frequently. If sauce looks too dry, add a little water. Place veal on a cutting board. Put sauce into a blender or food processor and process until smooth. Taste and adjust for seasoning. Slice meat and arrange on a large warm platter. Spoon sauce over meat. Serve immediately. Makes 6 to 8 servings.

Cold Veal in Tuna Fish Sauce

Vitello Tonnato

A classic, sensational dish. Great as an appetizer or main course.

1 (3-lb.) boneless veal roast,
   from top round or shoulder,
   firmly tied
1 carrot, chopped
1 celery stalk, chopped
1 onion, sliced

2 cups dry white wine
Tuna Fish Sauce, see below
Lemon slices
2 to 3 tablespoons capers
1 tablespoon chopped parsely

Tuna Fish Sauce:
1 (7-oz.) can tuna fish in olive oil
4 flat anchovy fillets
3 tablespoons capers

Juice of 1 lemon
3/4 cup olive oil
1 to 1-1/2 cups Mayonnaise, page 157

Trim fat from veal. Fill a large saucepan two-thirds full with water. Bring water to a boil. Add veal, carrot, celery, onion and wine. Cover pan and reduce heat. Simmer 2 to 2-1/2 hours or until meat is tender. Place meat and broth in a large bowl. Cover and refrigerate 3 to 4 hours. Prepare Tuna Fish Sauce. Cut cold veal into thin slices. Smear bottom of a large platter with Tuna Fish Sauce. Arrange veal slices, slightly overlapping, on top of sauce. Cover veal with remaining sauce. Cover platter and refrigerate overnight. When ready to serve, garnish with lemon slices, capers and parsley. Makes 6 to 8 servings.

Tuna Fish Sauce:
Put tuna fish, anchovies, capers, lemon juice and oil in a blender or food processor. Process to a fine paste. If sauce is too thick, add a few tablespoons veal broth. Combine tuna fish mixture and mayonnaise in a small bowl; mix well. Refrigerate until ready to use.

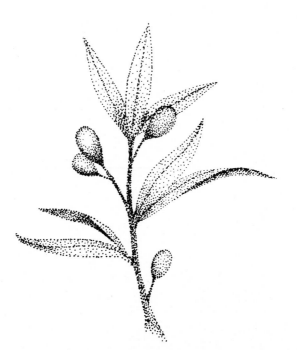

Cold Veal in Tuna Fish Sauce and Asparagus Salad, page 148

Stuffed Veal Roast   Photo on pages 180 and 181.

Arrosto di Vitello Farcito

Prosciutto complements the flavor of veal perfectly.

1 (2-1/2- to 3-1/2-lb.) boneless veal roast, from shoulder, top round or breast	Salt and freshly ground pepper to taste
2 garlic cloves, finely chopped	1/4 lb. prosciutto, page 6, sliced
Leaves from 2 sprigs fresh rosemary or 2 teaspoons dried rosemary	2 tablespoons butter
	3 tablespoons olive oil
	1 cup dry white wine
	1 chicken bouillon cube

Ask your butcher to open the veal roast and flatten it out. It should look like a large cutlet. Combine garlic and rosemary in a small bowl. Rub mixture on inner side of veal. Sprinkle with salt and pepper. Top with prosciutto slices. Roll up veal tightly. Secure rolled meat with string. Melt butter with oil in a large heavy casserole. When butter foams, add veal. Brown on all sides over medium heat. Add wine. Deglaze casserole by stirring to dissolve meat juices attached to bottom of casserole. When wine is reduced by half, reduce heat. Crumble bouillon cube into wine. Partially cover casserole. Cook veal 2 to 2-1/2 hours or until tender. Baste and turn meat several times during cooking. If sauce looks too dry, add a little more wine or water. Place veal on a cutting board and cool 5 minutes. Keep sauce warm. Slice meat and arrange on a warm platter. Taste and adjust sauce for seasoning, then spoon over meat. Serve immediately. Makes 6 to 8 servings.

Cutlets in Tomato & Pea Sauce

Cotolette in Umido con i Pisellini

A great dish for a cold winter night. Dunk Italian bread or Polenta, page 62, in the sauce.

2-1/2 to 3 cups Plain Tomato Sauce, page 161	1/2 cup freshly grated Parmesan cheese
6 veal cutlets	1/4 cup butter
2 eggs	3 tablespoons olive oil
Salt and freshly ground pepper to taste	1 small onion, finely chopped
1-1/2 cups dry unflavored breadcrumbs	1 carrot, finely chopped
	1 (10-oz.) pkg. frozen peas, thawed

Prepare Plain Tomato Sauce. Place cutlets between 2 pieces of waxed paper and pound until thin. When pounding meat do not use a straight up-and-down movement. Use a sliding action so meat is stretched more than flattened. Beat eggs with salt and pepper in a medium bowl. Combine breadcrumbs and Parmesan cheese in a small bowl. Spread on aluminum foil. Dip cutlets in beaten eggs, then coat with breadcrumb mixture. Press mixture onto cutlets with the palms of your hands. Let coated cutlets stand 10 to 15 minutes. Melt butter in a large skillet. When butter foams, add cutlets. Cook over medium heat 2 to 3 minutes on each side or until meat has a light-golden crust. Drain on paper towels. Heat oil in skillet. Add onion, carrot and celery. Sauté over medium heat until lightly browned. Stir in Plain Tomato Sauce and salt and pepper. Cook 5 to 6 minutes. Add cutlets and peas. Reduce heat and simmer 8 to 10 minutes. Taste and adjust for seasoning. Arrange cutlets and sauce on a warm platter. Serve hot. Makes 6 servings.

Variation

Substitute 3 chicken breasts, skinned, boned and split, page 90, for the veal cutlets.

Eggplants & Cutlets Parmigiana

Parmigiana di Melanzane e Cotolette

The complete dish can be prepared a day ahead and refrigerated.

3 cups Plain Tomato Sauce, page 161
2 medium eggplants
Salt and freshly ground pepper to taste
8 veal cutlets

Oil for frying
2 eggs
1-1/2 cups dry unflavored breadcrumbs
1-1/2 cups freshly grated Parmesan cheese

Prepare Plain Tomato Sauce. Peel eggplants. Cut lengthwise into 3/8-inch-thick slices. Sprinkle sliced eggplants with salt and place in a large dish. Set another large dish on top of eggplants and let stand 30 minutes. Salt draws out bitter juices from eggplants. Pat dry with paper towels. Place cutlets between 2 pieces of waxed paper and pound until thin. When pounding meat do not use a straight up-and-down movement. Use a sliding action so meat is stretched more than flattened. Heat oil in a large skillet. Add eggplants. Cook over medium heat until golden on both sides. Drain on paper towels. Beat eggs with salt and pepper in a medium bowl. Spread breadcrumbs on aluminum foil. Dip cutlets in beaten eggs, then coat with breadcrumbs. Press breadcrumbs onto cutlets with the palms of your hands. Let coated cutlets stand 10 to 15 minutes. Preheat oven to 400F (205C). Butter a 13" x 9" baking dish. Heat more oil in skillet. Add cutlets. Cook over medium heat 1 to 2 minutes on each side or until meat has a golden-brown crust. Drain on paper towels. Line bottom of buttered baking dish with half the eggplants. Arrange a layer of 4 veal cutlets over eggplants. Top with half the Plain Tomato Sauce. Sprinkle half the Parmesan cheese over tomato sauce. Make another layer ending with a layer of tomato sauce and Parmesan cheese. Bake 15 to 20 minutes or until cheese is melted and golden. Makes 8 servings.

Veal Cutlets Bologna-Style

Cotolette alla Bolognese

Fresh white truffles make this a dish fit for a king.

1/3 cup Chicken Broth, page 20, or
   canned chicken broth
4 veal cutlets
2 eggs
Salt and freshly ground pepper to taste
1 cup dry unflavored breadcrumbs

6 tablespoons freshly grated Parmesan cheese
1/4 cup butter
4 slices prosciutto, page 6, (about 2 oz.)
10 to 12 very thin slices white
   Italian truffles, if desired

Prepare Chicken Broth. Place cutlets between 2 pieces of waxed paper and pound until thin. When pounding meat do not use a straight up-and-down movement. Use a sliding action so meat is stretched more than flattened. Beat eggs with salt and pepper in a medium bowl. Combine breadcrumbs with 2 tablespoons Parmesan cheese in a small bowl. Spread on aluminum foil. Dip cutlets in beaten eggs, then coat with breadcrumb mixture. Press mixture onto cutlets with the palms of your hands. Let coated cutlets stand 10 to 15 minutes. Melt butter in a medium skillet. When butter foams, add cutlets. Cook over medium heat 2 to 3 minutes on each side or until cutlets have a light-golden crust. Place 1 slice prosciutto and 1 tablespoon Parmesan cheese on each cutlet. If using, add a few slices of white truffles. Add chicken broth. Cover skillet and reduce heat. Simmer 2 to 3 minutes or until cheese is melted. Place meat on a warm platter. Taste and adjust sauce for seasoning, then spoon over meat. Serve immediately. Makes 4 servings.

Mixed Boiled Meats

Bollito Misto

Serve with Green Sauce, page 159, and Sweet & Sour Sauce, page 160.

1 (2- to 2-1/2-lb.) cotechino sausage
3 to 3-1/2 lbs. beef brisket
3 to 4 large beef knuckle bones
1 large onion, quartered
2 celery stalks, chopped
2 carrots, chopped

2 or 3 parsley sprigs
1 tablespoon tomato paste or
   2 medium tomatoes, quartered
1 tablespoon salt
1 (2-1/2- to 3-lb.) chicken

Place cotechino sausage in a large bowl. Cover with cold water and soak overnight. Puncture sausage skin in several places with a fork. Place in a large saucepan. Cover with water. Bring water to a boil. Reduce heat and cover pan. Simmer sausage 1-1/2 to 2 hours, depending on size. While sausage is cooking, wash meat and bones thoroughly. Put everything except cotechino sausage and chicken, into a large stockpot. Add enough water to cover. Cover stockpot and bring water to a boil. Reduce heat. Simmer 2 to 2-1/2 hours, skimming off surface foam frequently. Add chicken. Simmer 1 to 1-1/2 hours longer or until meats are tender. Leave cotechino and other meats in broth until ready to serve. Place meats on a cutting board. Reserve broth for soups. Slice beef and cotechino sausage and carve chicken. Arrange everything on a large warm platter. Serve immediately. Makes 6 to 8 servings.

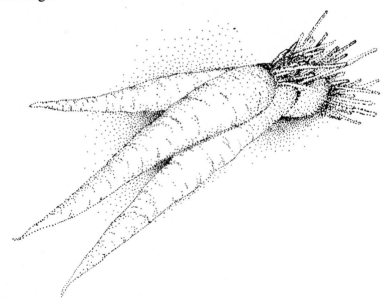

Florentine Steak

Bistecca alla Fiorentina

This steak has been a specialty of Florence for centuries and is famous all over Italy.

4 large T-bone steaks,
   about 1-1/2 inches thick

Salt and freshly ground pepper to taste
Olive oil

Preheat barbecue with wood or charcoal until very hot. Place steak on grill. Cook 4 to 5 minutes on 1 side or until dark brown. Turn steak carefully without puncturing it. Cook other side to desired doneness. Season with salt and pepper. Place steaks on individual dishes. Add a few drops of olive oil to each steak. Serve immediately. Makes 4 servings.

Family-Style Patties

Polpettine Casalinghe

Any leftover meat can be used for these crunchy patties.

3 slices white bread
1/2 cup milk
1-1/2 lbs. ground veal or beef
1/4 lb. mortadella or boiled ham,
   finely chopped
1/2 teaspoon freshly grated nutmeg

2 eggs
1/3 to 1/2 cup freshly grated Parmesan cheese
Salt and freshly ground pepper to taste
1 to 2 cups dry unflavored breadcrumbs
Oil for frying
2 eggs

Remove crust from bread. Tear bread into pieces. Combine bread and milk in a small bowl and squeeze together into a soft pulp. In a large bowl, combine veal or beef, mortadella or ham, bread-milk mixture, nutmeg, 2 eggs, Parmesan cheese and salt and pepper. Mix thoroughly. Spread breadcrumbs on aluminum foil. Beat 2 eggs with salt and pepper in a small bowl. Take a generous tablespoon of meat mixture, shape it into a small ball, then flatten between the palms of your hands. Dip patties into beaten eggs, then coat with breadcrumbs. Press breadcrumbs onto patties with the palms of your hands. Repeat until all mixture is used. Pour oil 1 inch deep in a large saucepan or skillet. Heat oil until a 1-inch cube of bread turns golden almost immediately. Using a slotted spoon, lower patties a few at a time into hot oil. Turn patties. When golden on both sides, remove from oil with slotted spoon. Drain on paper towels. Arrange drained patties on a warm platter. Serve hot. Makes 6 to 8 servings.

Meat Loaf Bologna-Style

Polpettone alla Bolognese

It can't always be steak so let this tasty dish solve the budget problem.

3 slices white bread
1/2 cup milk
2 lbs. chopped beef
2 eggs, lightly beaten
1/2 lb. pancetta, page 6, finely chopped
1/3 to 1/2 cup freshly grated
   Parmesan cheese
1/2 teaspoon freshly grated nutmeg
Salt and freshly ground pepper to taste

1/2 cup dry unflavored breadcrumbs
1/4 cup olive oil
1 medium onion, chopped
1 carrot, chopped
1 celery stalk, chopped
1 tablespoon chopped parsley
1/2 cup dry white wine
1-1/2 to 2 cups canned crushed
   Italian-style tomatoes

Preheat oven to 375F (190C). Remove crust from bread. Tear bread into pieces. Combine bread and milk in a small bowl and squeeze together into a soft pulp. In a large bowl, combine beef, bread-milk mixture, eggs, pancetta, Parmesan cheese, nutmeg and salt and pepper. Mix thoroughly. Shape mixture into a large flat sausage about 10 inches long and 3 inches thick. Coat meat loaf with breadcrumbs, pressing crumbs into meat lightly. Heat oil in a medium casserole. Add onion, carrot, celery and parsley. Sauté over medium heat until onion is pale yellow. Add meat loaf. Bake 20 to 25 minutes or until meat loaf is light golden. Add wine. Bake 10 minutes or until wine has evaporated. Add tomatoes. Bake 30 to 40 minutes longer, basting meat loaf with tomato sauce a few times during cooking. Cool meat loaf 5 to 10 minutes before slicing. Serve with 1 or 2 tablespoons sauce over each serving. Makes 6 servings.

Filet Mignons Piedmont-Style

Filetto alla Piemontese

Some of the best truffles in the world come from Piedmont and are widely used in local cooking.

4 slices white bread	**Salt and freshly ground pepper to taste**
6 tablespoons butter	**1 cup dry Marsala wine or sherry**
2 tablespoons anchovy paste	**1/3 cup whipping cream, if desired**
1 tablespoon olive oil	**10 to 12 very thin slices white**
4 filet mignons, 3/4 inch thick	**Italian truffles, if desired**

Remove crust from bread. Melt 3 tablespoons butter in a medium skillet. When butter foams, add bread. Cook over medium heat until golden on both sides. Place bread on a large ovenproof platter. Spread 1/2 tablespoon anchovy paste on each slice of bread. Keep platter warm in oven. Remove butter from skillet and clean with paper towels. Melt 3 tablespoons butter with oil. When butter foams, add filet mignons. Cook over medium-high heat 2 to 3 minutes on each side or until lightly browned. Season with salt and pepper. Add 1/2 cup Marsala or sherry. Deglaze skillet by stirring to dissolve meat juices attached to bottom of skillet. Cook meat over medium heat to preferred doneness. Place a filet mignon on each slice of bread. Keep warm. Add remaining Marsala or sherry and cream, if desired, to skillet. Stir over high heat until sauce has a medium-thick consistency. Spoon sauce over meat. Top with truffle slices, if desired. Serve immediately. Makes 4 servings.

Filet Mignons with Brandy, Cream & Peppercorns

Filetto con Brandy, Crema e Pepe Verde

From the Bacco Restaurant in Bologna comes this elegant, modern dish.

2 tablespoons ketchup	**3 tablespoons olive oil**
3 tablespoons Dijon mustard	**6 filet mignons, 3/4 inch thick**
4 to 5 drops Worcestershire sauce	**1/3 cup brandy**
2 tablespoons green peppercorns or	**1/2 cup whipping cream**
pinch red (cayenne) pepper	**Salt**
3 tablespoons butter	

In a small bowl, combine ketchup, mustard, Worcestershire sauce and green peppercorns or cayenne. Melt butter with oil in a large skillet. When butter foams, add meat. Cook over medium-high heat 1 to 2 minutes on each side or until lightly browned. Remove meat from skillet. Add brandy. Deglaze skillet by stirring to dissolve meat juices attached to bottom of skillet. Add ketchup-mustard mixture and cream; mix well. Return meat to skillet. Season with salt. Cook over medium heat to preferred doneness. Place meat on a warm platter. Spoon sauce over meat. Serve immediately. Makes 6 servings.

Filet Mignons Piedmont-Style

Beef Braised in Barolo Wine

Manzo al Barolo

This dish comes from the Piedmont region where fine wines and beef are produced.

2 garlic cloves, chopped
3 to 3-1/2 lbs. beef bottom round or chuck
Salt and freshly ground pepper to taste
2 fresh or dried bay leaves
Pinch of dried leaf thyme
4 to 5 cups Barolo wine or
  any full-bodied red wine

3 tablespoons butter
2 tablespoons olive oil
1 medium onion, finely chopped
1 carrot, finely chopped
1 celery stalk, finely chopped
1/2 lb. small white mushrooms

Rub garlic into meat. Season with salt and pepper. Place meat in a large bowl. Add bay leaves, thyme and enough wine to cover meat. Cover and refrigerate overnight. Drain meat, reserving marinade. Dry meat with paper towels. Melt 2 tablespoons butter with oil in a large heavy casserole. When butter foams, add meat. Brown meat on all sides over medium heat. Remove meat from casserole. Add onion, carrot and celery to casserole. Sauté until lightly browned. Return meat to casserole. Pour reserved marinade through a strainer over meat. Cover casserole and reduce heat. Simmer 2 to 2-1/2 hours or until meat is tender. Turn and baste meat often during cooking. Wash and dry mushrooms thoroughly and slice thin. Melt 1 tablespoon butter in a medium skillet. Sauté mushrooms over high heat until golden. Add mushrooms to meat and cook 5 minutes longer. Place meat on a cutting board and cool 5 minutes. If sauce is too thin, cook uncovered over high heat 5 to 10 minutes. Slice meat and arrange on a warm platter. Taste and adjust sauce for seasoning, then spoon over meat. Serve immediately. Makes 6 to 8 servings.

Beef Goulash

Gulasch di Manzo

This Trentino-Alto Adige dish has an Austrian influence because Alto Adige was once part of Austria.

1 cup Chicken Broth, page 20, or
  canned chicken broth
3 lbs. beef chuck
2 tablespoons butter
3 tablespoons olive oil
3 medium onions, thinly sliced
2 tablespoons red wine vinegar
1 teaspoon paprika

1 (28-oz.) can crushed Italian-style or
  whole tomatoes
1 garlic clove
1/2 teaspoon dried leaf marjoram
1/2 teaspoon crushed dried bay leaves
Grated zest of 1 lemon
Salt and freshly ground pepper to taste

Prepare Chicken Broth. Cut meat into 1-1/2- to 2-inch cubes. Melt butter and oil in a large heavy skillet. When butter foams, add onions. Sauté over medium heat until pale yellow. Add vinegar and paprika. Stir until vinegar has evaporated. Add meat. Brown lightly on all sides. Stir in tomatoes, garlic, marjoram, bay leaves, lemon zest, chicken broth and salt and pepper. Cover skillet and reduce heat. Simmer 1-1/2 to 2 hours or until meat is tender. Stir occasionally during cooking. Serve hot. Makes 6 to 8 servings.

How to Make Beef Braised in Barolo Wine

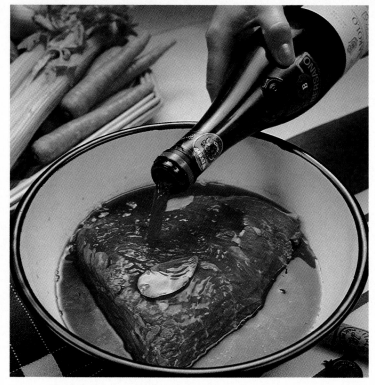

1/Add enough wine to cover meat.

2/Pour reserved marinade through a strainer over meat.

Beef Braised in Champagne

Manzo allo Champagne

Champagne turns an ordinary pot roast into an elegant and delicious dish.

1/2 cup all-purpose flour	1 medium onion, finely chopped
3 lbs. beef bottom or top round	1 celery stalk, finely chopped
1/4 cup butter	2 cups dry champagne or dry white wine
1 tablespoon olive oil	1 tablespoon tomato paste
1 carrot, finely chopped	1/2 cup whipping cream

Place flour on aluminum foil. Roll meat in flour. Melt butter with oil in a large heavy casserole. When butter foams, add meat. Brown on all sides over medium heat. Add carrot, onion and celery. Sauté over medium heat until lightly browned. Pour champagne or white wine over meat; stir well. Cook uncovered over medium heat until liquid is reduced by half. Stir in tomato paste. Cover and reduce heat. Simmer 2 to 2-1/2 hours or until meat is tender. Turn and baste meat often during cooking. Place meat on a cutting board. Put sauce in a blender or food processor and process to a paste. Return sauce to pan. Add cream. Stir over high heat 1 to 2 minutes or until sauce has a medium-thick consistency. Taste and adjust for seasoning. Cut meat into thin slices. Arrange slices on a warm platter. Spoon sauce over meat. Serve immediately. Makes 6 to 8 servings.

Vegetables

The Etruscans belonged to an ancient civilization that lived in northern Italy. Their love of the soil and knowledge of irrigation and fertilization made them devoted and expert farmers. The Romans inherited this love of the land from the Etruscans. They developed and enjoyed many new varieties of vegetables. Since then, agriculture has been one of Italy's national resources. Maybe that is why Italians cook vegetables better than anyone else. Their farmers have been growing vegetables longer and their produce is some of the world's finest.

One of the extraordinary sights in an Italian open market is its vegetable stalls. There you will find colorful mounds of vegetables and fruit still fresh from the farmer's patch. The Italian housewife inspects all this abundance with a critical eye. She touches, smells, compares and sometimes bargains. Satisfied with her purchase, she goes home to cook the freshest possible produce.

In an Italian meal, vegetables are always present. Many times meat is omitted from a family meal in favor of one or two types of vegetables.

In selecting fresh vegetables, look for bright colors and shiny skins without bruises. A good

Menu

Risotto with Prawns, page 68
Fried Sole Fillets, page 76
Tomatoes with Piquant
Green Sauce, page 133
Jam Tart, page 168
Tocai Friulano or *Dry Chenin Blanc

*California wine

vegetable should be firm to the touch. When selecting zucchini or string beans, choose the smallest available. Asparagus should be bright green with compact tips. Choose broccoli with tender but firm stalks and no signs of yellow flowers within the buds. Carrots should be bright orange, small and smooth. Avoid cauliflowers with blemishes and look for a compact head. Eggplants are best if they are not too large, have firm flesh and bright-green leaves. Always select mushrooms with tightly closed caps.

Use your vegetables as soon as possible after purchase to take advantage of their freshness. Vegetables are at their best when undercooked. Prolonged cooking will result in vitamin and texture loss. Vitamin-packed vegetables are essential to good nutrition.

To serve a meal without a vegetable is almost like hanging a painting without a frame. Choose from the real-life palette of colors and you'll see that their taste and appearance will enhance even the simplest of meals.

The patient wait for seasonal vegetables becomes especially rewarding when the first tiny peas or tender asparagus arrive on the market. When buying seasonal vegetables the good cook knows she is buying the freshest and most flavorful produce. She also knows she is saving money. Once you have bought the best possible produce, very little is needed to enhance its flavor. Why cover tender green asparagus with a rich filling sauce? Why not boil it briefly then dress it simply with olive oil and lemon juice? Or sprinkle it with cheese, dot with a little butter and broil until the cheese is melted.

Italians love raw vegetables. One of the favorite ways to eat them is dipped in olive oil and salt. What could be simpler than that? This practice must have had a humble origin, but today some of the best restaurants serve vegetables this way.

A relative newcomer to Italian cuisine is the tomato. Tomatoes were introduced into Europe from North America around the year 1500. They were treated with suspicion and used like an exotic garden plant for many years. Today we can hardly imagine Italian cuisine without the tomato. A plump, sun-ripened tomato sliced and dressed with fresh basil and olive oil is delicious.

Peperonata

Peperonata

In Bologna, Peperonata is served with Mixed Boiled Meats, page 120, and Green Sauce, page 159.

1/3 cup olive oil	5 medium tomatoes, chopped
2 medium onions, thinly sliced	1 tablespoon tomato paste
5 sweet peppers, green and red,	Salt and freshly ground pepper to taste
seeded, cut into strips	1/4 cup red wine vinegar

Heat oil in a large skillet. Add onions and peppers. Sauté over medium heat until onions are light golden and peppers have softened. Add tomatoes, tomato paste and salt and pepper. Cover and cook over medium heat 30 to 35 minutes, stirring occasionally. Add vinegar and mix well. Cook uncovered 10 minutes longer. Taste and adjust for seasoning. Serve hot or at room temperature. Makes 3-1/2 to 4 cups or 8 to 10 servings.

Baked Asparagus with Parmesan Cheese

Asparagi alla Parmigiana

Select small asparagus with firm, tightly closed tips for this authentic dish from Parma.

2-1/2 lbs. asparagus   **3 tablespoons butter**
1/2 cup freshly grated Parmesan cheese

Preheat oven to 350F (175C). Butter a 13'' x 9'' baking dish. Cut off tough asparagus ends. Using a sharp knife or potato peeler, peel outer skin from asparagus. Tie asparagus together in 1 or 2 bunches with string or rubber bands. Pour cold salted water 2 to 3 inches deep in an asparagus cooker, tall stockpot or old coffeepot. Place asparagus upright in water. Bring water to a boil. Cover and cook over high heat 6 to 8 minutes, depending on size. Drain on paper towels; remove string or rubber bands. Arrange drained asparagus slightly overlapping in buttered baking dish. Sprinkle with Parmesan cheese and dot with butter. Bake 10 to 15 minutes or until cheese is melted. For a light-golden topping, put baked asparagus briefly under a hot broiler. Serve hot. Makes 4 to 6 servings.

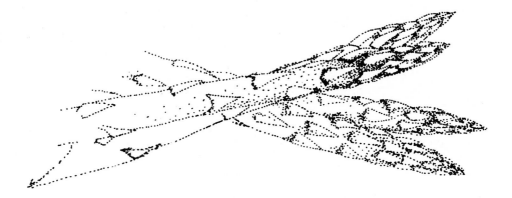

Broccoli with Garlic & Anchovies

Broccoli in Padella con Acciughe

An excellent and simple vegetable dish in the true Italian manner.

2 lbs. broccoli   **3 flat anchovy fillets, mashed**
1/4 cup olive oil   **Salt and freshly ground pepper to taste**
3 garlic cloves, chopped   **3 tablespoons chopped parsley**

Cut off tough bottoms from broccoli. Using a sharp knife or potato peeler, peel outer skin. Divide broccoli and wash thoroughly under cold running water. Fill a large saucepan two-thirds full with salted water. Bring water to a boil. Add broccoli and reduce heat. Simmer 5 to 8 minutes or until stalks are tender. Drain on paper towels. Heat oil in a large skillet. Stir in garlic and anchovies. Add drained broccoli. Season with salt and pepper and sprinkle with parsley. Turn broccoli gently and cook over medium heat 3 to 5 minutes. Place broccoli on a warm platter and spoon sauce over vegetable. Serve hot. Makes 6 to 8 servings.

Friggione

Friggione

There is no translation for Friggione. The word implies a range of ingredients fried together.

5 to 6 tablespoons olive oil
4 potatoes, peeled, cut into small pieces
2 large onions, thinly sliced
2 red or green sweet peppers,
   seeded, cut into strips

Salt and freshly ground pepper to taste
2 cups canned crushed Italian-style or
   whole tomatoes

Heat oil in a large skillet. Add potatoes, onions and peppers. Season with salt and pepper. Cook uncovered over low heat 30 minutes, stirring several times. Press tomatoes through a food mill or a sieve, page 161, to remove seeds. Add tomato pulp to skillet. Cook uncovered over medium heat 25 to 30 minutes or until mixture reduces to a medium-thick consistency. Add salt and pepper to taste. Makes 4 to 6 servings.

Sautéed Spinach

Spinaci Saltati

Serve this tasty spinach with Veal Chops Milan-Style, page 111, or Stuffed Veal Roast, page 118.

2 lbs. spinach
1 teaspoon salt
4 to 5 tablespoons olive oil

2 garlic cloves, chopped
3 flat anchovy fillets, chopped
Salt and freshly ground pepper to taste

Wash spinach thoroughly in several changes of cold water. Discard stems and bruised or tough leaves. Put wet spinach into a large saucepan; add 1 teaspoon salt. Cover pan. Cook over medium heat 10 to 12 minutes or until spinach is tender. Drain well; cool slightly. Squeeze spinach to remove as much moisture as possible. Heat oil in a large skillet. Add garlic and anchovies. Sauté over medium heat about 1 minute. Before garlic changes color, add spinach. Season with salt and pepper. Cook 2 to 3 minutes, stirring constantly. Serve hot. Makes 6 servings.

Eggplants with Parsley & Garlic

Melanzane al Funghetto

Capers add extra zest to this excellent dish.

2 medium eggplants
Salt
1/3 cup olive oil
3 garlic cloves, finely chopped

3 tablespoons chopped parsley
2 tablespoons capers, if desired
Salt and freshly ground pepper to taste

Peel eggplants. Cut lengthwise into 1-inch thick slices. Sprinkle sliced eggplants with salt and place in a large dish. Set another large dish on top of eggplants and let stand 30 minutes. Salt draws out bitter juices from eggplants. Pat dry with paper towels. Cut into cubes. Heat oil in a large skillet. Add eggplants and garlic. Cook over medium heat 15 minutes, turning several times. Add parsley, capers if desired, and salt and pepper. Cook 5 minutes longer. Taste and adjust for seasoning. Serve hot or at room temperature. Makes 6 servings.

Baked Stuffed Zucchini

Zucchine Ripiene al Forno

Stuffed zucchini are excellent, but filling. Serve them with a plain roast or as a luncheon.

8 to 10 medium, firm zucchini
White Sauce, see below
3 tablespoons chopped parsley
1/4 lb. mortadella or boiled ham, chopped

2 tablespoons fresh unflavored breadcrumbs
Salt and freshly ground pepper to taste
2 tablespoons freshly grated Parmesan cheese

White Sauce:
2 tablespoons butter
2 tablespoons all-purpose flour
1 cup hot milk

1/2 teaspoon grated nutmeg
3 tablespoons freshly grated Parmesan cheese
Salt to taste

Preheat oven to 350F (175C). Butter a 13'' x 9'' baking dish. Wash zucchini. Fill a medium saucepan two-thirds full with salted water. Bring water to a boil. Add zucchini. Cook over medium heat 5 to 10 minutes, depending on size. Zucchini should be barely tender. Drain. Rinse under cold running water. Pat dry with paper towels. Prepare White Sauce. Trim ends off zucchini and slice zucchini in half lengthwise. Scoop out pulp with a small spoon. Combine zucchini pulp, parsley, mortadella or boiled ham, breadcrumbs and salt and pepper in a medium bowl. Add White Sauce; mix well. Taste and adjust for seasoning. Fill zucchini shells with pulp mixture and sprinkle with Parmesan cheese. Place stuffed zucchini in buttered baking dish. Bake 20 to 25 minutes or until zucchini have a light-golden crust. Serve hot. Makes 6 servings.

White Sauce:
Melt butter in a medium saucepan. When butter foams, whisk in flour. Cook over medium heat 2 or 3 minutes. Do not let flour brown. Whisk in hot milk quickly to prevent lumps. Cook sauce 2 to 3 minutes longer, whisking constantly. Add nutmeg, Parmesan cheese and salt; blend well. Sauce should have a medium-thick consistency.

Zucchini with Vinegar

Zucchine Fritte all'Aceto

This is the vegetable dish that won the hearts of my students.

1-1/2 lbs. zucchini, smallest available
Oil for frying
1 cup all-purpose flour

Salt and freshly ground pepper to taste
3 tablespoons red wine vinegar

Wash and dry zucchini. Trim ends. Slice zucchini into 1/4-inch rounds. Pour oil 1 inch deep in a large saucepan. Heat oil until a 1-inch cube of bread turns golden brown almost immediately. Place zucchini slices a few at a time in a sieve and sprinkle with flour. Shake off excess flour. Using a slotted spoon, lower zucchini into hot oil. When golden on both sides, remove from oil with slotted spoon. Drain on paper towels. When all zucchini are cooked, place in a salad bowl. Season with salt and pepper and add vinegar. Toss gently. Serve at room temperature. Makes 4 to 6 servings.

How to Make Baked Stuffed Zucchini

1/Scoop out pulp from zucchini with a small spoon.

2/Fill zucchini shells with pulp mixture and sprinkle with Parmesan cheese.

Zucchini in Batter

Zucchine Fritte con la Pastella

Serve this crunchy vegetable dish with fried meats or roasts.

1-1/2 lbs. zucchini, smallest available
2 cups water
2 cups all-purpose flour

Oil for frying
Salt to taste

Wash and dry zucchini. Trim ends. Cut zucchini into sticks 2 inches long and 1/2 inch thick. Put water in a medium bowl. Gradually sift flour into water, beating constantly. Batter should have the consistency of mayonnaise. If too thin, add a little more flour; if too thick, add more water. Batter can be prepared a few hours ahead. Pour oil 2 inches deep in a large saucepan or deep-fryer. Heat oil to 375F (190C) or until a 1-inch cube of bread turns golden brown almost immediately. Dip zucchini sticks into batter. Using a slotted spoon, lower zucchini sticks a few at a time into hot oil. When golden on all sides, remove from oil with slotted spoon. Drain on paper towels. Arrange drained zucchini on a warm platter and season with salt. Serve hot. Makes 6 to 8 servings.

Mushrooms Parmigiana

Parmigiana di Funghi

If you prefer a mild and sweet flavor, use the Italian fontina cheese.

Plain Tomato Sauce, page 161   **1/3 cup freshly grated Parmesan cheese**
3 lbs. small white mushrooms
1/4 cup butter
1/4 lb. Italian fontina or Danish
  fontina cheese, thinly sliced, or
  1 cup freshly grated Parmesan cheese

Preheat oven to 350F (175C). Butter an 11" x 7" baking dish. Prepare Plain Tomato Sauce. Wash and dry mushrooms thoroughly and cut into wedges. Melt butter in a large skillet. When butter foams, add mushrooms. Sauté over high heat until golden. Spoon some tomato sauce into buttered baking dish. Cover sauce with a layer of mushrooms and top with slices of fontina cheese or some Parmesan cheese. Repeat layers, finishing with tomato sauce. Sprinkle 1/3 cup Parmesan cheese over last layer of tomato sauce. Bake 25 to 30 minutes. Let stand a few minutes before serving. Makes 6 to 8 servings.

Mushrooms with Marsala Wine & Cream

Funghi con Marsala e Panna

The look and aroma of these mushrooms are mouthwatering.

3 lbs. small white mushrooms   **1/2 cup dry Marsala wine or cream sherry**
3 tablespoons butter   **1/2 cup whipping cream**
1 tablespoon olive oil   **Salt and freshly ground pepper to taste**

Wash and dry mushrooms thoroughly and cut into slices. Melt butter with oil in a large skillet. When butter foams, add mushrooms. Sauté over high heat until golden. Stir in Marsala or sherry. Cook over high heat until liquid is reduced by half, stirring occasionally. Add cream and cook a few minutes longer. Season with salt and pepper. Serve hot. Makes 8 servings.

Mushrooms with Parsley & Garlic

Funghi Triffolati

Serve this with other vegetable dishes for an unusual appetizer.

1-1/2 lbs. small white mushrooms   **1/4 cup chopped parsley**
2 tablespoons butter   **3 garlic cloves, chopped**
2 tablespoons olive oil   **Salt and freshly ground pepper to taste**

Wash and dry mushrooms thoroughly and cut into slices. Melt butter with oil in a large skillet. When butter foams, add mushrooms. Sauté over high heat until golden. Add parsley, garlic and salt and pepper; cook 1 minute longer. Taste and adjust for seasoning. Serve hot or at room temperature. Makes 6 to 8 servings.

Baked Tomatoes   Photo on pages 180 and 181.

Pomodori al Forno

A colorful accompaniment for a simple fish dish.

6 tomatoes
1/3 cup olive oil
1/4 cup chopped parsley
2 garlic cloves, chopped
2 tablespoons capers

1/3 cup freshly grated Parmesan cheese
1/3 cup dry unflavored breadcrumbs
Salt and freshly ground pepper to taste
2 tablespoons olive oil

Preheat oven to 350F (175C). Wash and dry tomatoes. Cut in half. Using a small spoon, remove seeds from tomatoes. Drain tomatoes cut-side down on paper towels 15 to 20 minutes. Combine 1/3 cup oil, parsley, garlic, capers, Parmesan cheese, breadcrumbs and salt and pepper in a medium bowl. Divide mixture between tomato halves. Place tomatoes in a 13" x 9" baking dish. Spoon 2 tablespoons oil over tops of tomatoes into dish. Bake 25 to 30 minutes or until filling is crisp and golden. Serve hot. Makes 6 to 8 servings.

Tomatoes with Piquant Green Sauce   Photo on page 94.

Pomodori alla Salsa Verde

A great summer vegetable dish to add elegance to a simple barbecue.

4 large tomatoes
2 eggs
1/3 cup olive oil
1 slice white bread
1-1/2 cups loosely packed parsley
2 garlic cloves

2 tablespoons capers
4 flat anchovy fillets
1 teaspoon mustard
Juice of 1 lemon
Salt and freshly ground pepper to taste

Wash and dry tomatoes. Cut in half. Using a small spoon, remove seeds from tomatoes. Drain tomatoes cut-side down on paper towels 15 to 20 minutes. Put eggs in a small saucepan and cover with cold water. Cook 8 minutes from the time water begins to boil. Remove yolks from eggs. In a blender or food processor, combine egg yolks, oil, bread, parsley, garlic, capers, anchovies, mustard, lemon juice and salt and pepper. Blend to a paste, the consistency of mayonnaise. If too thin, add another slice of white bread; if too thick, add 2 or 3 tablespoons oil. Filling can be prepared several hours ahead. Fill tomato halves with sauce and refrigerate until ready to use. Makes 8 servings.

Braised Curly Cabbage

Verze Affogate

A tasty winter vegetable that is perfect with Pork Loin with Garlic & Rosemary, page 104.

1 (2-lb.) curly cabbage
3 tablespoons olive oil
1/4 lb. pancetta, page 6,
   cut into 4 slices and diced
2 garlic cloves, crushed

1 sprig fresh rosemary or
   1 teaspoon dried rosemary
Salt and freshly ground pepper to taste
1/2 cup dry white wine

Wash and dry cabbage; shred. Heat oil in a large skillet. Add pancetta, garlic and rosemary. Sauté over medium heat until lightly browned. Stir in cabbage and salt and pepper. Cover skillet and reduce heat. Simmer 20 minutes, stirring a few times during cooking. Add wine and simmer uncovered 15 minutes longer. Serve hot. Makes 6 to 8 servings.

Red Cabbage with Smoked Ham & Apples

Cavolo Rosso con Prosciutto Affumicato e Mele

This dish comes from Trentino-Alto Adige where smoked meat is a main ingredient in local cooking.

1 (2- to 2-1/2-lb.) red cabbage
2 tablespoons butter
2 tablespoons olive oil
1 large onion, thinly sliced

1/4 lb. smoked ham, chopped
1 cup red wine
2 apples, peeled, diced
Salt and freshly ground pepper to taste

Remove bruised outer leaves from cabbage. Cut cabbage into thin slices. Melt butter with oil in a large skillet. When butter foams, add onion. Sauté until pale yellow. Add ham and cabbage. Cook uncovered over high heat 10 minutes. Add wine. Cook until wine is reduced by half. Add apples and season with salt and pepper. Reduce heat to medium. Cover and cook 10 minutes longer. Serve warm. Makes 6 to 8 servings.

String Beans with Cream

Fagiolini alla Panna

Use the freshest and smallest beans for a light and delicate dish.

1-1/2 lbs. string beans
3 tablespoons butter
1/2 cup whipping cream
1 egg yolk, lightly beaten

2 tablespoons whipping cream
Juice of 1 lemon
Salt and freshly ground pepper to taste
1/3 cup freshly grated Parmesan cheese

Snap ends off beans. Wash beans. Fill a large saucepan two-thirds full with salted water. Bring water to a boil. Add beans. Cook over high heat 5 to 10 minutes or until tender but firm. Drain on paper towels. Melt butter in a large skillet. When butter foams, add 1/2 cup cream and bring to a boil. Add drained beans. Cook over medium heat 2 to 3 minutes. Combine egg yolk, 2 tablespoons cream, lemon juice and salt and pepper in a small bowl. Taste and adjust for seasoning. Add mixture to skillet and mix rapidly. Add Parmesan cheese and stir to coat beans. Serve immediately. Makes 6 servings.

Cauliflower in Batter

Cavolfiore Fritto con la Pastella

Vegetables fried in this flour and water batter are crisp and light.

1 (2-1/2- to 3-lb.) cauliflower	**2 eggs, lightly beaten**
1-1/2 cups water	**Oil for frying**
2 cups all-purpose flour	**Salt to taste**

Remove leaves from cauliflower. Slice cauliflower in half. Fill a large saucepan two-thirds full with salted water. Bring water to a boil. Add cauliflower. Cook over high heat 15 to 20 minutes or until tender. Drain on paper towels; cool. Put 1-1/2 cups water in a medium bowl. Gradually sift flour into water, beating constantly. Beat in eggs. Batter should be the consistency of mayonnaise. Batter can be prepared a few hours ahead. Pour oil 2 inches deep in a large saucepan or deep-fryer. Heat oil to 375F (190C) or until a 1-inch cube of bread turns golden brown almost immediately. Detach florets from cauliflower. Dip florets into batter. Using a slotted spoon, lower a few at a time into hot oil. Turn cauliflower. When golden on all sides, remove from oil with slotted spoon. Drain on paper towels. Arrange drained cauliflower on a warm platter and season with salt. Serve hot. Makes 6 to 8 servings.

Baked Fennel with Butter & Cheese

Finocchi al Forno con Burro e Formaggio

If you have never tasted fennel, be adventurous and try this dish.

4 large fennels	**1/4 cup butter**
Salt and freshly ground pepper to taste	**1/3 cup freshly grated Parmesan cheese**

Preheat oven to 350F (175C). Butter a 13" x 9" baking dish. Cut off long stalks and bruised leaves from fennels. Slice end off bulbous base. Wash fennels thoroughly. Cut into quarters. Fill a large saucepan two-thirds full with water. Bring water to a boil. Add fennels. Cook over high heat 10 to 15 minutes or until tender but firm. Drain fennels on paper towels. Arrange slightly overlapping in buttered baking dish. Season with salt and pepper. Dot generously with butter and sprinkle with Parmesan cheese. Bake 15 minutes or until fennel is tender and cheese is melted. Serve hot. Makes 6 to 8 servings.

Baked Onions

Cipolle al Forno

These refreshingly light onions are perfect for lamb and pork roasts.

5 tablespoons olive oil　　　　　　　　**Salt and freshly ground pepper to taste**
4 large yellow onions

Preheat oven to 375F (190C). Put 3 tablespoons oil in an 11"x 7" baking dish. Cut onions in half horizontally and place cut-side up in baking dish. Season with salt and pepper. Drizzle remaining oil over each onion. Bake 40 to 60 minutes, depending on size. Onion tops should be light golden. Serve hot. Makes 4 servings.

Sweet & Sour Little Onions

Cipolline Agro-Dolci

These onions are the ideal accompaniment to any roast.

3 (10-oz.) or 2 (16-oz.) pkgs.　　　　**1/4 cup packed brown sugar**
**　frozen little onions, thawed**　　　　**1/4 cup red wine vinegar**
1/4 cup butter　　　　　　　　　　　**Salt to taste**

Drain onions thoroughly on paper towels. Melt butter in a large skillet. When butter foams, add drained onions. Sauté over medium heat 5 to 8 minutes or until onions begin to color. Add brown sugar and stir to coat onions. Add vinegar and salt. Cook 2 to 3 minutes longer. Sauce should be thick and coat onions. Serve hot. Makes 8 to 10 servings.

Peas with Prosciutto

Piselli al Prosciutto

Peas cooked this way also make a marvelous, light sauce for noodles.

1 cup Chicken Broth, page 20, or　　　**3 tablespoons olive oil**
**　canned chicken broth**　　　　　　　**1 medium onion, thinly sliced**
3 lbs. fresh peas or 3 (10-oz.) pkgs.　　**1/4 lb. prosciutto, page 6, diced**
**　frozen small peas, thawed**　　　　　**Salt and freshly ground pepper to taste**

Prepare Chicken Broth. Shell fresh peas. Bring broth to a boil in a medium saucepan. Add peas. Cook 5 to 10 minutes, depending on size. Drain peas. Heat oil in a small skillet. Add onion. Sauté over medium heat until pale yellow. Add prosciutto and peas. Sauté 3 to 4 minutes. Season with salt and pepper. Serve hot. Makes 6 to 8 servings.

Stuffed Artichokes   Photo on pages 180 and 181.

Carciofi Ripieni

It takes a little time and patience to prepare these artichokes but they are well worth it.

4 large artichokes
1 lemon
4 slices white bread
1/2 cup olive oil
1/3 cup chopped parsley

3 garlic cloves, chopped
Salt and freshly ground pepper to taste
Water
3 to 4 tablespoons olive oil

Cut off artichoke stems; slice and reserve. Remove and discard hard outer leaves of artichokes. Cut sharp tips off remaining leaves with scissors. Slice off about 1/2 inch from top end of each artichoke. Open artichokes gently with your hands. Remove fuzzy chokes with a knife or melon-baller. Wash artichokes under cold running water. Slice lemon in half and rub over cut tops of artichokes. Set artichokes with cut part down on paper towels. Remove crusts from bread. Chop bread into small pieces and place in a medium bowl. Add 1/2 cup oil, parsley, garlic and salt and pepper. Mix well. Arrange mixture between artichoke leaves and in centers. Place artichokes and reserved stems in a large saucepan. Pour water about 1 inch deep in pan. Add 3 to 4 tablespoons oil. Bring water to a boil. Reduce heat to medium and cover pan. Cook artichokes 40 to 60 minutes, depending on size. If water evaporates, add a little more. There should be 4 to 5 tablespoons of sauce left in pan. If too much liquid is left, uncover pan and boil liquid down. Spoon sauce over artichokes and stems. Serve hot. Makes 4 servings.

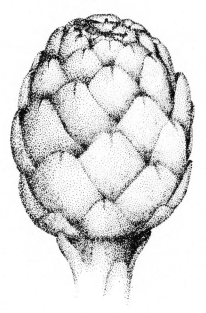

How to Make Stuffed Artichokes

1/Cut sharp tops off leaves with scissors.

2/Slice off about 1/2 inch from top end of artichoke.

3/Remove fuzzy chokes with a melon-baller.

4/Arrange stuffing between leaves and in centers.

Roasted Potato Balls   Photo on page 94.

Patatine Arrosto

These potatoes are beautiful to look at and delicious to eat.

8 large Idaho potatoes, peeled
2 tablespoons butter
2 tablespoons olive oil
2 sprigs fresh rosemary or
   2 teaspoons dried rosemary

2 garlic cloves
Salt and freshly ground pepper to taste

Using a melon-baller, scoop potatoes into balls. Fill a large saucepan half full with salted water. Bring water to a boil. Add potato balls and boil 1 minute. Drain on paper towels. Melt butter with oil in a large skillet. When butter foams, add drained potatoes, rosemary, garlic and salt and pepper. Cook over medium heat, turning frequently. When potatoes are golden, remove garlic and fresh rosemary, if using. Serve immediately. Makes 4 to 6 servings.

Potato Cake

Pinza di Patate

A different way to serve potatoes.

8 large Idaho potatoes
3 eggs
Salt to taste
3 tablespoons butter, melted

3 tablespoons olive oil
1/3 cup freshly grated Parmesan cheese
2 tablespoons all-purpose flour
1 egg yolk, lightly beaten

Butter an 8-inch cake pan with a removable bottom. Fill a large saucepan two-thirds full with water. Add potatoes. Bring to a boil. Boil gently until potatoes are tender. Preheat oven to 350F (175C). Peel and mash potatoes while hot. Beat 3 eggs with salt in a large bowl. Beat in melted butter and oil. Add mashed potatoes, Parmesan cheese and flour; mix well. Put potato mixture into buttered pan and smooth top with a spatula. Brush top with beaten egg yolk. Bake 20 to 25 minutes or until top is golden. Unmold potato cake and place on a warm platter. Serve immediately. Makes 6 to 8 servings.

Potato balls can be boiled ahead and sautéed at the last moment.

How to Make Roasted Potato Balls

1/Use a melon-baller to scoop potatoes into balls.

2/Turn potatoes often while cooking.

Buttered Carrots   Photo on pages 180 and 181.

Carote Dorate al Burro

The humble carrot shines in this simple dish.

1 lb. small carrots
2 quarts water
1 tablespoon salt
3 tablespoons butter

2 tablespoons sugar
Salt to taste
1 tablespoon chopped parsley

Cut carrots into sticks 3 inches long. Fill a medium saucepan half full with salted water. Bring water to a boil. Add carrots. Cook over medium heat 2 to 3 minutes or until carrots are barely tender. Drain carrots on paper towels. Melt butter in a large skillet. When butter foams, add carrots and sauté over medium heat 2 to 3 minutes. Add sugar and mix well. Season with salt. Garnish with parsley. Serve immediately. Makes 6 servings.

I am always mystified when people ask me how much garlic or how many herbs I put in my salad dressing. I suppose the false notion that Italian salad dressing should contain every possible herb and seasoning started with the television commercials that advertise bottled or packaged dressing. Nothing could be simpler, tastier and less complicated than an Italian salad dressing. There is never any discussion among Italians on how to dress a salad. It is and always has been a combination of salt, olive oil and wine vinegar. But if you prefer, pepper can be added and lemon juice can replace vinegar.

Often my students want to know exactly how much oil and vinegar to put in a dressing. The amount will depend on the quantity and kind of salad. As a general rule, be generous with olive oil but stingy with vinegar. Don't forget to taste the dressing before adding it to your salad. I can give you as many proportions of salad dressing as there are salads. But, ultimately, you have to decide. Basically it is the same concept that guides all Italian cooking, whether you come from

Risotto Milan-Style, page 69
Veal Shanks Milan-Style, page 114
Fennel Salad, page 144
Sweet Fried Cream, page 178
Nebbiolo d'Alba or *Charbono

*California wine

Veneto or Sicily. The best and freshest ingredients should stand on their own merits. A green or mixed salad needs only excellent olive oil and good wine vinegar to be outstanding.

Salad in Italy is never served before the first course. It is always served after the main course. There are at least two reasons for this. Salad is meant to clean and refresh the palate for cheese, fruit or dessert that follows. Another reason is that the sharpness of the vinegar used in salad dressing would destroy the taste of wine served with the main course.

The salad that follows an important meal should be kept simple. A green salad, or a mixed salad containing tomatoes, carrots and radishes would be appropriate. Or you could serve a single-vegetable salad using asparagus or string beans. A salad made with mixed cooked vegetables is too substantial to serve with a special meal. Instead, serve it with cheese or eggs to make a light family lunch or supper.

The abundant harvests of spring and summer, with string beans, tomatoes and asparagus bring joy and color to your salads and table. Fall and winter vegetables such as fennel and cauliflower will help you create more unusual salads.

Make sure your vegetables are thoroughly washed and dried before dressing them. To dry lettuce, place it in a kitchen cloth. Hold the corners of the cloth together and shake energetically. Then pat individual lettuce leaves dry with paper towels. Dress your salad only when ready to serve it or it will become soggy and wilted.

I am a firm believer that all good cooking begins in the market. Whether you cook Italian, Chinese or French food, the selection of first-quality ingredients will greatly determine the success of your dish. This is especially true for vegetables and salads because those ingredients will be prepared with a minimum of sauces or dressing. Very often you need not pay extra money for first-quality ingredients. You only need to recognize and select the best from what is available.

Cucumber Salad with Sour Cream

Insalata di Cetrioli e Crema Acida

This cucumber salad is dressed with sour cream and paprika in the manner of bordering Austria.

3 or 4 cucumbers
1/3 cup dairy sour cream

Pinch of paprika
Salt and freshly ground pepper to taste

Peel cucumbers and slice into 1/4-inch rounds. Place sliced cucumbers in a large sieve and let stand 1 hour. Cucumbers will release their bitter juices. Pat dry with paper towels. Place cucumbers in a salad bowl. Combine sour cream, paprika and salt and pepper in a small bowl. Add to cucumbers; mix gently. Serve at room temperature. Makes 4 to 6 servings.

Variation

Cucumber Salad (Insalata di Cetrioli): Prepare cucumbers and place in a salad bowl. Season with salt and pepper. Sprinkle with a pinch of paprika. Add 1/3 cup olive oil and 1 to 2 tablespoons red wine vinegar; toss gently. Serve at room temperature.

Fennel Salad

Insalata di Finocchi

Follow your main course with this crunchy salad.

2 large fennels
1 tablespoon chopped parsley
1 garlic clove, finely chopped

Salt and freshly ground pepper to taste
3 to 4 tablespoons olive oil
1 tablespoon red wine vinegar

Cut off long stalks and bruised leaves from fennels. Slice ends off bulbous bases. Wash fennels thoroughly. Cut into quarters, then horizontally into thin slices. Place in a salad bowl. Add parsley and garlic. Season with salt and pepper. Add oil and vinegar; toss gently. Serve at room temperature. Makes 6 servings.

Cauliflower Salad

Cavolfiore in Insalata

A great winter salad when lettuce is scarce and expensive.

1 (2- to 2-1/2-lb.) cauliflower
Salt and freshly ground pepper to taste

1/3 cup olive oil
1 to 2 tablespoons red wine vinegar

Remove leaves from cauliflower. Slice cauliflower in half. Fill a large saucepan two-thirds full with water. Bring water to a boil. Add cauliflower. Cook over high heat 15 to 20 minutes or until tender. Drain on paper towels; cool. Detach florets from cauliflower and place in a salad bowl. Season with salt and pepper. Add oil and vinegar; toss gently. Serve at room temperature. Makes 6 servings.

Cooked Mixed Vegetable Salad

Insalata Cotta

A colorful addition to any meal.

1 large fennel
1/4 lb. small string beans
Salt and freshly ground pepper to taste
2 medium potatoes

2 or 3 carrots
1 tablespoon chopped parsley
1/4 cup olive oil
1 to 2 tablespoons red wine vinegar

Cut off long stalks and bruised leaves from fennel. Slice end off bulbous base. Wash fennel thoroughly. Cut into quarters. Fill a medium saucepan half full with salted water. Bring water to a boil. Add fennel. Cook over high heat 10 to 15 minutes or until tender but firm. Drain on paper towels; cool. Trim and wash beans. Fill a small saucepan half full with salted water. Bring water to a boil. Add beans. Cook over high heat 5 to 10 minutes or until tender but firm. Drain on paper towels; cool. Thinly slice fennel. Place string beans and fennel in a salad bowl. Fill a medium saucepan two-thirds full with salted water. Bring water to a boil. Add potatoes and carrots. Cook over high heat 10 to 15 minutes. Test carrots. Remove when tender but firm. Drain on paper towels; cool. Slice into 1/4-inch rounds. Add carrots to salad bowl. Cook potatoes 10 to 15 minutes longer or until tender but firm. Peel while hot. Cool 20 to 25 minutes. Cut into 1/4-inch slices. Add potatoes to salad bowl. Sprinkle vegetables with parsley. Season with salt and pepper. Add oil and vinegar; toss gently. Serve at room temperature. Makes 6 servings.

How to Make Fennel Salad

1/Cut off long stalks and bruised leaves from fennels.

2/Cut bulbous base into quarters.

Tuna Fish & Bean Salad

Insalata di Tonno e Fagioli

You will find this humble salad appetizing and surprisingly filling.

1-1/2 to 2 cups dried white kidney or
  Great Northern beans
1 large red onion
2 (7-oz.) cans Italian tuna fish, or
  other tuna in olive oil

Salt and freshly ground pepper to taste
5 tablespoons olive oil
2 tablespoons red wine vinegar

Place beans in a large bowl. Add enough cold water to cover and let stand overnight. Drain and rinse beans thoroughly. Place beans in a large saucepan. Add enough cold water to cover. Cover and bring to a boil. Reduce heat. Simmer 50 to 60 minutes, stirring occasionally. Drain beans and let cool. Place in a salad bowl. Slice onion into thin strips. Place in a small bowl with enough cold water to cover. Let stand 1 hour, changing water several times. Drain onion. Pat dry with paper towels. Add to beans. Drain oil from tuna. Flake tuna. Add to salad bowl. Season with salt and pepper. Add oil and vinegar; toss gently. Serve at room temperature. Makes 6 servings.

Tomato Salad

Insalata di Pomodori

Ripe tomatoes, the fragrance of basil and the goodness of olive oil capture the essence of summer.

4 large tomatoes　　　　　　　　　　　**8 to 10 fresh basil leaves**
Salt and freshly ground pepper to taste　**1/4 cup olive oil**

Wash and dry tomatoes. Cut into slices or wedges. Place tomatoes in a salad bowl. Season with salt and pepper. Tear basil leaves into pieces and add to tomatoes. Add oil; toss gently. Serve slightly chilled. Makes 4 to 6 servings.

Zucchini Salad

Zucchine in Insalata

Select zucchini that are small, firm and a shiny green.

1-1/2 lbs. zucchini　　　**1/3 cup olive oil**
Juice of 2 lemons　　　　**2 tablespoons chopped parsley**
Salt to taste　　　　　　**2 garlic cloves, finely chopped**

Wash zucchini. Fill a large saucepan two-thirds full with salted water. Bring water to a boil. Add zucchini. Cook over medium heat 5 to 10 minutes, depending on size. Zucchini should be barely tender. Rinse under cold running water. Pat dry with paper towels. Slice zucchini into 1/4-inch rounds. Place in a salad bowl. Combine lemon juice and salt in a small bowl. Add oil, parsley and garlic; mix until blended. Taste and adjust for seasoning. Pour dressing over zucchini. Serve slightly chilled. Makes 6 to 8 servings.

Cooked Onion Salad

Insalata di Cipolle Cotte

The onion has been worshipped, acclaimed and vilified but our cooking would not be the same without it!

5 or 6 medium, yellow onions　　**Salt and freshly ground pepper to taste**
6 tablespoons olive oil　　　　　**1 to 2 tablespoons red wine vinegar**

Preheat oven to 350F (175C). Cut ends off onions and peel. Fill a large saucepan half full with water. Bring water to a boil. Add onions and bring water back to a boil. Cook over high heat 2 to 3 minutes. Drain onions and rinse under cold running water. Pat dry with paper towels. Put 2 tablespoons oil in a medium casserole, add onions. Bake 40 to 50 minutes or until golden. Remove from oven and cool. Slice onions. Place in a salad bowl. Season with salt and pepper. Add 1/4 cup oil and vinegar; toss gently. Serve at room temperature. Makes 4 to 6 servings.

Cabbage & Mushroom Salad

Insalata Appetitosa

This vitamin-packed salad is perfect for days when you don't feel like cooking.

1/2 small white cabbage	**Juice of 1 lemon**
1/2 small red cabbage	**1 teaspoon mustard**
1/2 lb. small white mushrooms	**Salt and freshly ground pepper to taste**
1/4 lb. Swiss cheese	**1/4 cup olive oil**

Remove bruised outer leaves from cabbage. Cut cabbage into thin slices. Wash and dry mushrooms thoroughly. Cut into thin slices. Cut Swiss cheese into thin strips. Place all ingredients in a salad bowl. Combine lemon juice, mustard and salt and pepper in a small bowl. Add olive oil; mix until blended. Taste and adjust for seasoning. Pour dressing over salad; toss gently. Serve at room temperature. Makes 6 servings.

Asparagus Salad   Photo on page 117.

Asparagi in Insalata

Fresh, tender asparagus is at its best with this simple oil-and-lemon dressing.

2 lbs. asparagus	**1/3 cup olive oil**
Juice of 1 large lemon	**2 hard-cooked eggs**
Salt to taste	

Cut off tough asparagus ends. Using a sharp knife or potato peeler, peel outer skin from asparagus. Tie asparagus together in 1 or 2 bunches with string or rubber bands. Pour cold salted water 2 to 3 inches deep in an asparagus cooker, tall stockpot or old coffeepot. Place asparagus upright in water. Bring water to a boil. Cover and cook over high heat 6 to 8 minutes, depending on size. Remove string or rubber bands. Place 2 or 3 layers of paper towels on a large platter and place cooked asparagus on top to drain. Refrigerate until ready to serve. A few hours before serving, remove asparagus from refrigerator. Combine lemon juice and salt in a small bowl. Add oil; mix until blended. Taste and adjust for seasoning. Remove paper towels from platter. Arrange asparagus neatly. Spoon dressing over vegetable. Remove yolks from hard-cooked eggs. Press yolks through a strainer over aparagus. Serve at room temperature. Makes 4 to 6 servings.

Variation   Photo on page 94.

String Bean Salad with Oil & Lemon (Fagiolini all'Olio e Limone): Substitute 2 pounds cooked string beans for the asparagus. Use the juice of 2 lemons and 1/2 cup olive oil.

How to Make Cabbage & Mushroom Salad

1/Cut cabbage into thin slices.

2/Gently toss salad.

Mixed Salad   Photo on page 79.

Insalata Mista

A mixed salad is almost always present at the end of an Italian meal.

1 large fennel	**2 medium tomatoes**
2 carrots	**Salt to taste**
1 large red or green sweet pepper	**3 to 4 tablespoons olive oil**
1 small lettuce	**1 tablespoon red wine vinegar**

Cut off long stalks and bruised leaves from fennel. Slice end off bulbous base. Wash and dry fennel. Cut into quarters, then horizontally into thin slices. Cut carrots into thin rounds. Wash and dry pepper. Cut in half and remove pith and seeds. Cut into very thin strips. Discard any bruised leaves from lettuce. Wash remaining leaves under cold running water. Pat dry with paper towels. Tear leaves into medium pieces. Place all vegetables in a salad bowl. Wash and dry tomatoes. Cut into slices and add to salad bowl. When ready to serve, season with salt. Add oil and vinegar; toss gently. Serve slightly chilled. Makes 4 to 6 servings.

Eggs &

$\mathcal{A}$n egg should have no nationality. What does one country do with an egg that another can't? After all, hard-cooked, scrambled or fried eggs can be eaten in many places around the world. Other special ways of cooking eggs are peculiar to certain countries. Americans eat eggs with bacon. The French have savory omelets. Italians have the *frittata*.

A frittata can be made with herbs, vegetables, cheese, fish or meat. It can also be made with jam or honey. It is said that the Romans used to mix eggs with honey. Perhaps they were the originators of the first frittata. A frittata is perfect for a light evening meal. It is great for a luncheon. It is excellent served cold for a snack or appetizer. In this chapter you will find four frittatas. But don't stop there, try your own variations. Don't forget about leftover meat and vegetables. They go perfectly in a frittata.

Eggs are easy to prepare and economical. They are a complete food with vitamins, sodium, protein, calcium and fat. When an egg is fresh, the yolk should be compact and the white should be transparent and tight around the yolk. Eggs are often eaten hard-cooked in a salad. They can be

$\mathcal{M}enu$

Zucchini Frittata, page 154
Cooked Mixed Vegetable Salad,
page 144
Italian Cheeses
Fresh Fruit
Orvieto or *Chenin Blanc

*California wine

fried or baked with vegetables or cheese. One of my favorite ways is eggs poached in a light tomato sauce.

Think of a lovely sunny day. A day you want to spend outside, gardening, swimming or reading a good book. Cooking is the last thing you want to do. But you have a family to feed—so make a frittata. Maybe the one with fresh tomatoes and basil. It will only take 10 to 15 minutes. Serve it with a green salad, crusty Italian bread and chilled white wine. Then leave the dishes and go out again, pleasantly satisfied. Enjoy the rest of your beautiful summer day.

Sauces

There are very few *basic* Italian sauces, but the sauces served with pasta are innumerable. These cannot be termed basic sauces because they are used only in specific dishes.

Italian cooks believe the pleasure of eating is increased by preserving the individual characteristics of ingredients. For this reason, the good Italian cook avoids the overuse of sauces. Sauces for meat, poultry and fish are usually only pan juices enriched with a little wine, broth or cream.

Basic common sense and a natural inclination toward balance guides the good Italian cook. If one course of a meal has a sauce, the chances are other courses will not. Very often sauces clash rather than complement each other. Keep this in mind when you plan a menu.

Here are a few important points to remember about Italian sauces: Use them sparingly. A sauce should enhance a dish, not overpower it. With a few exceptions, Italian sauces are best when not overcooked. Who has not been served, at one time or another, a tomato sauce so thick and dark that it tasted more like tomato paste? Overcooked sauces lose their freshness and individuality. Often Italian sauces consist simply of fresh herbs and vegetables. They are either sautéed briefly or left uncooked.

Only Mayonnaise and Basic White Sauce have precise quantities and definite techniques. The remaining sauces are an extension of the cook's style. Once you understand Italian ingredients and the best way to combine their flavors, you can relax. You will gradually begin to improvise. Finally, you will learn to cook like Italians do, not with formulas but with feelings.

Fried Eggs with Fontina Cheese

Uova Fritte con la Fontina

A light, yet filling dish that can replace meat for an impromptu supper.

3 to 4 tablespoons butter
8 eggs
Salt and freshly ground pepper to taste

8 slices Italian fontina or Swiss cheese
(about 1/4 lb.)

Melt butter in a large skillet. When butter foams, break eggs into skillet. Season with salt and pepper. Cook over medium heat about 1 minute. Place 1 slice fontina or Swiss cheese over each egg. Cover skillet and cook 6 to 8 minutes or until eggs are firm and cheese is melted. Place 2 eggs on each of 4 serving plates. Serve immediately. Makes 4 servings.

Eggs with Tomatoes

Uova alla Diavola

A great low-budget meal.

2 cups Plain Tomato Sauce, page 161
3 tablespoons butter
1 tablespoon olive oil
2 medium onions, thinly sliced

Salt and freshly ground pepper to taste
6 large eggs
8 tablespoons freshly grated Parmesan cheese

Prepare Plain Tomato Sauce. Melt butter with oil in a large skillet. When butter foams, add onions. Sauté over medium heat until pale yellow. Add tomato sauce and season with salt and pepper. Break eggs into skillet and cook about 1 minute. Spoon a generous tablespoon Parmesan cheese over each egg. Cover skillet and reduce heat. Simmer 5 to 6 minutes or until eggs are firm and cheese is melted. Place 2 eggs on each of 3 serving plates. Spoon tomato sauce around eggs. Serve immediately. Makes 3 servings.

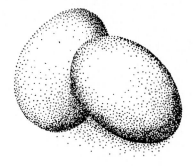

Baked Eggs with Spinach

Uova al Forno con gli Spinaci

In Italy, egg dishes are often served for the light evening meal.

2 to 2-1/2 lbs. fresh spinach or
** 2 (10-oz.) pkgs. frozen spinach**
1 teaspoon salt
Salt and freshly ground pepper to taste

8 eggs
10 tablespoons freshly grated
** Parmesan cheese**

Wash fresh spinach thoroughly in several changes of cold water. Discard stems and bruised or tough leaves. Put wet spinach into a large saucepan; add 1 teaspoon salt. Cover pan. Cook over medium heat 10 to 12 minutes or until spinach is tender. Cook frozen spinach according to package directions. Drain well; cool slightly. Squeeze spinach to remove as much moisture as possible. Preheat oven to 350F (175C). Butter an 11'' x 7'' baking dish. Spread spinach in buttered baking dish. Make 8 small wells in spinach and break an egg into each well. Season with salt and pepper. Cover each egg with a generous tablespoon Parmesan cheese. Bake 8 to 10 minutes or until eggs are firm and cheese is melted. Place 2 eggs and some spinach on each of 4 serving plates. Serve immediately. Makes 4 servings.

How to Make Eggs with Tomatoes

1/Sprinkle Parmesan cheese over each egg.

2/Cook until eggs are firm and cheese is melted.

Baked Eggs with Peperonata

Uova al Tegamino con la Peperonata

Eggs and leftover Peperonata become a light lunch or supper.

1-1/3 cups Peperonata, page 127
8 eggs

Salt and freshly ground pepper to taste
1/4 cup freshly grated Parmesan cheese

Prepare Peperonata. Preheat oven to 350F (175C). Butter 4 ramekins. Put 1/3 cup Peperonata in each ramekin and break 2 eggs into each one. Season with salt and pepper. Sprinkle 1/2 tablespoon Parmesan cheese over each egg. Bake 8 to 10 minutes or until eggs are firm and cheese is melted. Serve immediately. Makes 4 servings.

Variation

Baked Eggs with Prosciutto (Uova al Forno con Prosciutto): Omit Peperonata. Line each ramekin with 2 or 3 slices prosciutto, page 6, or boiled ham.

Zucchini Frittata

Frittata di Zucchine

It is important to use a heavy skillet to make a perfect frittata.

6 large eggs
Salt and freshly ground pepper to taste
1/3 cup freshly grated Parmesan cheese
1/4 cup butter
1 tablespoon olive oil

1 medium onion, thinly sliced
3 zucchini, finely sliced
2 tablespoons chopped parsley
2 garlic cloves, chopped

Beat eggs with salt and pepper in a medium bowl. Beat in Parmesan cheese. Melt 3 tablespoons butter with oil in a heavy 8- or 10-inch skillet. When butter foams, add onion. Sauté over medium-low heat about 1 minute. Add zucchini, parsley and garlic. Sauté 3 to 4 minutes or until lightly browned. Remove zucchini mixture with a slotted spoon. Stir into egg mixture. Melt remaining butter in skillet. When butter foams, add egg mixture. Cook over medium heat 5 to 6 minutes or until bottom of frittata is lightly browned. Place a large plate on top of skillet and turn frittata onto plate. Slide inverted frittata back into skillet. Cook 4 to 5 minutes longer. Slide frittata onto a warm serving dish. Cut into 4 wedges. Serve hot or at room temperature. Makes 4 servings.

Ricotta Cheese, Onion & Parsley Frittata

Frittata di Ricotta, Cipolla e Prezzemolo

Leftover frittata makes an excellent snack or a super sandwich.

6 large eggs
Salt and freshly ground pepper to taste
1 cup ricotta cheese
2 tablespoons chopped parsley

3 tablespoons butter
1 tablespoon olive oil
1 medium onion, thinly sliced

Beat eggs with salt and pepper in a medium bowl. Beat in ricotta cheese and parsley. Melt 2 tablespoons butter with oil in a heavy 8- or 10-inch skillet. When butter foams, add onion. Sauté over medium heat until pale yellow. Remove onion with a slotted spoon. Stir into egg mixture. Melt remaining butter in skillet. When butter foams, add egg mixture. Cook over medium heat 5 to 6 minutes or until bottom of frittata is lightly browned. Place a large plate on top of skillet and turn frittata onto plate. Slide inverted frittata back into skillet. Cook 4 to 5 minutes longer. Slide frittata onto a warm serving dish. Cut into 4 wedges. Serve hot or at room temperature. Makes 4 servings.

Variation

Onion Frittata (Frittata di Cipolle): Substitute 1/3 cup freshly grated Parmesan cheese for the ricotta cheese and omit parsley. Use 2 tablespoons olive oil and 2 large onions.

Zucchini Frittata and Tomato Sauce Bologna-Style, page 157

Tomato & Basil Frittata

Frittata al Pomodoro e Basilico

The variations for frittatas are endless. Only your imagination will set the limit.

4 medium tomatoes
6 large eggs
Salt and freshly ground pepper to taste
1/3 cup freshly grated Parmesan cheese
3 tablespoons butter

1 tablespoon olive oil
2 medium onions, thinly sliced
2 garlic cloves, chopped
6 to 8 fresh basil leaves, finely chopped

Peel, seed and dice tomatoes, as for Penne with Hot Pepper & Tomatoes, page 42. Beat eggs with salt and pepper in a medium bowl. Beat in Parmesan cheese. Melt 2 tablespoons butter with oil in a heavy 8- or 10-inch skillet. Add onions and garlic. Sauté over medium heat until onions are pale yellow. Add tomatoes and basil. Cook 5 to 6 minutes or until tomato juices have evaporated. Remove tomato mixture with a slotted spoon. Stir into egg mixture. Melt remaining butter in skillet. When butter foams, add egg mixture. Cook over medium heat 5 to 6 minutes or until bottom of frittata is lightly browned. Place a large plate on top of skillet and turn frittata onto plate. Slide inverted frittata back into skillet. Cook 4 to 5 minutes longer. Slide frittata onto a warm serving dish. Cut into 4 wedges. Serve hot or at room temperature. Makes 4 servings.

Fried Eggs with Asparagus Parma-Style

Uova Fritte con Asparagi alla Parmigiana

A light treat when asparagus is plentiful.

2-1/2 lbs. asparagus
3 tablespoons butter

8 eggs
Salt and freshly ground pepper to taste

Cut off tough asparagus ends. Using a sharp knife or potato peeler, peel outer skin from asparagus. Tie asparagus together in 1 or 2 bunches with string or rubber bands. Pour cold salted water 2 to 3 inches deep in an asparagus cooker, tall stockpot or old coffeepot. Place asparagus upright in water. Bring water to a boil. Cover and cook over high heat 6 to 8 minutes, depending on size. Drain on paper towels; remove string or rubber bands. Divide asparagus into 4 bundles. Place on 4 serving dishes. Melt butter in a large skillet. When butter foams, break eggs into skillet. Season with salt and pepper. Cook over medium heat until firm. Place 2 eggs on top of each asparagus bundle. Serve immediately. Makes 4 servings.

Mayonnaise

Maionese

One of the secrets of homemade mayonnaise is to have all ingredients and utensils at room temperature.

2 egg yolks
Salt to taste

1-1/2 cups olive oil
1 tablespoon lemon juice

Place egg yolks in a round-bottom bowl. Add salt. Beat until yolks are pale yellow. Very slowly beat in a few drops of oil. Do not add oil too quickly or Mayonnaise will curdle. Add remaining oil very slowly, beating constantly. Beat in lemon juice. Taste and adjust for seasoning. Refrigerate. Bring to room temperature before using. Makes 1-1/2 cups of Mayonnaise.

Variation

Stir in 2 tablespoons Pesto Sauce, page 159, or 2 tablespoons Green Sauce, page 159, for green mayonnaise to serve with fish. Sauces must be at room temperature before adding to mayonnaise.

Tomato Sauce Bologna-Style   Photo on page 155.

Salsa di Pomodoro alla Maniera di Bologna

In summer, when tomatoes are at their best, make a large quantity of this excellent sauce and freeze it.

3 lbs. ripe plum tomatoes or
   overripe regular tomatoes
1/2 cup olive oil
2 carrots, finely chopped
2 celery stalks, finely chopped

1 medium onion, finely chopped
1/2 cup loosely packed fresh basil
1/2 cup loosely packed parsley
Salt and freshly ground pepper to taste

Cut tomatoes into large pieces. Heat oil in a large saucepan. Add tomatoes, carrots, celery, onion, basil, parsley and salt and pepper. Bring to a boil. Reduce heat to medium. Cook uncovered 30 to 40 minutes or until sauce reaches a medium-thick consistency. Taste and adjust for seasoning. Press everything through a food mill and back into saucepan. Cook 20 to 30 minutes longer. Makes 4-1/2 cups of sauce.

If mayonnaise curdles, beat an additional egg yolk until pale yellow. Gradually beat curdled mayonnaise into egg yolk.

Basic White Sauce

Salsa Balsamella

Whether French or Italian in origin, this sauce is vital to many Italian dishes.

Use these ingredients	To Make			
	3/4 cup	**1-1/2 cups**	**2-1/4 cups**	**3-3/4 cups**
milk	1 cup	2 cups	3 cups	5 cups
butter	2 tablespoons	4 tablespoons	6 tablespoons	10 tablespoons
all-purpose flour	2 tablespoons	4 tablespoons	6 tablespoons	10 tablespoons
salt	to taste	to taste	to taste	to taste

Bring milk almost to a boil; set aside. Melt butter in a medium saucepan. When butter foams, stir in flour. Let mixture bubble gently over low heat 1 to 2 minutes, stirring constantly. Do not let mixture brown. Whisk in milk all at once. Whisk until smooth. Season with salt. Simmer 3 to 5 minutes, whisking constantly until sauce has a medium-thick consistency. Reduce or increase cooking time for a thinner or thicker sauce. If not using immediately, rub surface of sauce with 1/2 tablespoon softened butter to prevent a skin from forming.

White Sauce can be prepared two or three days ahead and refrigerated. When cooled it will set. Add a few tablespoons of milk and stir over low heat to return sauce to its original consistency.

Pesto Sauce

Pesto

If you plan to freeze the sauce, add the cheese after the sauce has thawed.

3 cups loosely packed fresh basil
3/4 cup olive oil
1/4 cup pine nuts
3 garlic cloves

1 teaspoon salt
1/2 cup freshly grated Parmesan cheese
3 tablespoons Romano pecorino cheese or
 Parmesan cheese

Put basil, oil, pine nuts, garlic and salt into a blender or food processor. Process until smooth. Pour sauce into a small bowl. Add Parmesan cheese and Romano pecorino cheese or extra Parmesan cheese. Mix to blend. Taste and adjust for seasoning. Makes 1 cup of sauce.

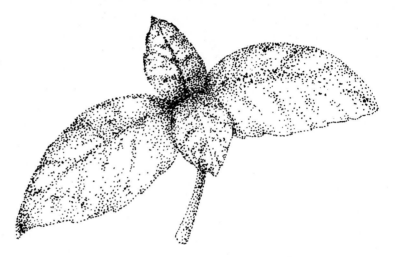

Green Sauce

Salsa Verde

The perfect accompaniment for Mixed Boiled Meats, page 120.

1 slice white bread
2 tablespoons red wine vinegar
2 cups loosely packed parsley
2 garlic cloves

4 flat anchovy fillets
1 tablespoon capers
1/2 cup olive oil
Salt and freshly ground pepper to taste

Remove crust from bread. Tear bread into pieces and place in a small bowl. Pour vinegar over bread. Let stand 10 minutes. Put into a blender or food processor. Add parsley, garlic, anchovies, capers and oil. Process until smooth. Place sauce in a small bowl. Season with salt and pepper. Refrigerate. Serve at room temperature. Makes 3/4 cup of sauce.

Variation

Substitute lemon juice for the vinegar and serve with fish.

Bolognese Meat Sauce

Ragù alla Bolognese

The recipe for this classic sauce has been in my family for generations.

1/4 cup butter
2 tablespoons olive oil
1 medium onion, finely chopped
1 carrot, finely chopped
1 celery stalk, finely chopped
1/4 lb. pancetta, page 6, finely chopped

1-1/2 lbs. ground veal
Salt and freshly ground pepper to taste
1 cup dry white wine
1 (28-oz.) can crushed Italian-style tomatoes
1/2 cup milk

Melt butter with oil in a large saucepan. When butter foams, add onion, carrot, celery and pancetta. Sauté over medium heat until lightly browned. Add veal. Cook and stir until meat is no longer pink. Season with salt and pepper. Increase heat and stir in wine. Cook until wine has evaporated. Press tomatoes through a food mill or sieve, opposite, to remove seeds. Stir tomato pulp into veal mixture. Cover and reduce heat. Simmer 1 to 1-1/2 hours or until sauce reaches a medium-thick consistency. Stir occasionally during cooking. Add milk and cook 5 minutes longer. Makes 2-1/2 to 3 cups of sauce.

Sweet & Sour Sauce

Salsa Agrodolce

A classic Bolognese sauce that dates back to the sixteenth century.

2 tablespoons tomato paste
3/4 cup water
2 tablespoons butter
1 tablespoon olive oil
1/3 cup chopped parsley

4 garlic cloves, finely chopped
1 teaspoon all-purpose flour
1 tablespoon sugar
2 tablespoons red wine vinegar
Salt and freshly ground pepper to taste

Mix tomato paste and water in a small bowl. Melt butter with oil in a small saucepan. When butter foams, add parsley and garlic. Sauté over low heat until garlic begins to color. Stir in flour and sugar. Stir in vinegar and diluted tomato paste; mix until blended. Season with salt and pepper. Cook over medium heat 4 to 5 minutes, stirring frequently. Makes 1/2 cup of sauce.

How to Make Bolognese Meat Sauce

1/Press tomatoes through a food mill to remove seeds.

2/Simmer sauce until it is medium-thick.

Plain Tomato Sauce

Salsa di Pomodoro Semplice

Many recipes in this book will need some of this sauce.

1 tablespoon olive oil
1 (28-oz.) can crushed Italian-style tomatoes

Salt and freshly ground pepper to taste

Heat oil in a medium saucepan. Press tomatoes through a food mill or sieve, above, to remove seeds. Add tomato pulp to saucepan. Simmer uncovered 15 to 20 minutes. Season with salt and pepper. Makes about 2 cups of sauce.

Only the pulp and juice of a fruit or vegetable pass through a food mill. Skin, seeds and any tough material remain behind.

Desserts

*T*here is no doubt most Italians would rather miss dessert than a first course. After all, at the end of an Italian meal you don't have room for a rich dessert. Fresh fruit, on the other hand, will refresh the palate and end the meal on a pleasant, light note.

For centuries, Italy has produced some of the best desserts in Europe. Anyone who has walked through Italian cities and looked at pastry shops will agree. Rich and elaborate desserts are generally store-bought and served on special occasions. On Sundays, many families go to pastry shops to buy *paste miste,* assorted pastries to complete the Sunday meal.

Italy also has an incredible number of less-complicated desserts called *dolci casalinghi,* family cakes. These are usually items like jam or fruit tarts or fruit cakes. They are simple to make and do not involve difficult techniques. Most keep well for several days and are not overly sweet. When an unexpected guest arrives, a slice of moist apple cake or crisp walnut pie is served with the ritual cup of espresso coffee.

Many families have their own version of a particular cake. The recipe is handed down from generation to generation and the cake is considered a

Menu

Roasted Peppers, page 16
Penne with Hot Pepper
& Tomatoes, page 42
Little Pork Bundles, page 105
Baked Onions, page 136
Rice Cake, page 173
Ghemme or *Pinot Noir

*California wine

showpiece. Generally this cake is prepared for a family celebration or a religious holiday.

Because elaborate desserts do not play an important role in Italian home-cooking, most desserts in this chapter are easy to make. A few require a little more skill and patience.

In 1960, I arrived in the United States as the young bride of an American doctor. I was suddenly faced with desserts served at the end of almost every meal. In spite of the rich Bolognese cuisine, I never had a weight problem. So I enthusiastically explored these new, rich and creamy desserts. Of all the desserts, my favorite was American apple pie. I had apple pie every day, sometimes twice a day, sometimes with ice cream on top. And slowly I began to grow—sideways. I finally realized that all my clothes were too small and decided to weigh myself. I was 20 pounds overweight. Apple pie did what pasta couldn't.

It is important to know what kind of dessert to serve on specific occasions. For a formal, elegant dinner choose an impressive dessert. In doing so, keep in mind the dinner that precedes it. Decide on a dessert that will complement it.

You should also keep in mind the season. In spring and summer, lighter desserts are preferable, such as Strawberry Mousse or Maria Angela's Meringue Cake. Fall and winter allow you to indulge in richer desserts like Italian Rum Cake, Chocolate Mousse or the mouthwatering Little Corner Restaurant Cake. For an informal get-together you will never go wrong with Sweet Pasta Fritters. Pile them on an attractive plate so adults and children can serve themselves.

Let's not forget fresh fruit. It should always be present in an Italian dinner. In winter, slice oranges and serve them with a liqueur sauce—or poach some ripe pears in red wine. In summer, choose the best strawberries, raspberries, peaches and apricots. Arrange them beautifully on a large platter and you will have an eye-catching instant dessert.

Cantaloupes with Marsala Wine

Meloni al Marsala

This is an elegant, refreshing way to start or end a meal.

2 cups strawberries
3 small cantaloupes

1 cup sugar
1 cup dry Marsala wine or sherry

Wash and hull strawberries. Cut cantaloupes in half and remove seeds. With a round melon-baller, scoop out pulp; reserve cantaloupe shells. Put melon balls and strawberries into a large bowl. Add 1/2 cup sugar and Marsala or sherry; mix well. Refrigerate several hours. Sprinkle cantaloupe shells with remaining sugar and refrigerate. When ready to serve, fill cantaloupe shells with marinated cantaloupes and strawberries. Spoon some juice over fruit. Serve chilled. Makes 6 servings.

Apple Fritters

Frittelle di Mele

Most countries have an apple fritter dessert. This is the northern Italian version.

4 large apples	**6 tablespoons all-purpose flour**
3/4 cup sugar	**Pinch of salt**
5 tablespoons rum or other liquor	**Oil for frying**
2 eggs, separated, room temperature	**1/3 cup sugar**
3/4 cup milk	

Core and peel apples and cut into rounds. Combine apples, 3/4 cup sugar and rum or other liquor in a large bowl. Cover bowl and let apples marinate 2 to 3 hours. Beat egg yolks in a medium bowl. Beat in milk. Gradually sift in flour, mixing constantly. Beat egg whites and salt in a small bowl until stiff. Fold beaten whites into batter. Pour oil 2 inches deep in a large saucepan or deep-fryer. Heat oil to 375F (190C) or until a 1-inch cube of bread turns golden brown almost immediately. Dip apple rounds into batter. Using a slotted spoon, lower a few rounds at a time into hot oil. Turn fritters. When golden on both sides, remove from oil with slotted spoon. Drain on paper towels. Arrange drained fritters on a platter. Sprinkle with 1/3 cup sugar. Serve hot. Makes 4 to 6 servings.

Rice Fritters

Frittelle di Riso

You will eat these fritters as fast as you can make them.

2 cups milk	**3 eggs, separated, room temperature**
1/2 cup arborio rice, page 6, or	**6 tablespoons all-purpose flour**
other short-grain rice	**3 tablespoons rum**
2 tablespoons butter	**Pinch of salt**
1/2 cup granulated sugar	**Oil for frying**
Grated zest of 1 lemon	**Powdered sugar**

Bring milk to a boil in a medium saucepan. Add rice and cook uncovered over medium heat 10 minutes. Stir in butter, granulated sugar and lemon zest. Cook 15 to 20 minutes longer, stirring mixture several times. When rice is done, all milk should be absorbed. Place rice mixture in a bowl to cool slightly. When rice is warm, add egg yolks, flour and rum; mix well. Beat egg whites and salt in a medium bowl until stiff. Fold beaten whites into rice mixture. Pour oil 2 inches deep in a large saucepan or deep-fryer. Heat oil to 375F (190C) or until a 1-inch cube of bread turns golden brown almost immediately. Drop batter a few tablespoonfuls at a time into hot oil. Turn fritters. When golden on both sides, remove from oil with a slotted spoon. Drain on paper towels. Arrange drained fritters on a platter. Sprinkle with powdered sugar. Serve hot. Makes 6 to 8 servings.

Cheese Fritters

Frittelle di Ricotta

Watch these Cheese Fritters puff up into little golden balls.

4 eggs
1/2 cup granulated sugar
Few drops of vanilla extract
2 teaspoons baking powder

1 lb. ricotta cheese
1 cup all-purpose flour
Oil for frying
Powdered sugar

In a large bowl, beat eggs until fluffy. Add granulated sugar, vanilla and baking powder; mix well. Mix in ricotta cheese. Fold in flour a little at a time. Cover bowl and let batter stand at room temperature 1 hour. Pour oil 2 inches deep in a large saucepan or deep-fryer. Heat oil to 375F (190C) or until a 1-inch cube of bread turns golden brown almost immediately. Drop batter a few tablespoonfuls at a time into hot oil. Turn fritters. When golden on both sides, remove from oil with a slotted spoon. Drain on paper towels. Arrange drained fritters on a platter. Sprinkle with powdered sugar. Serve hot. Makes 8 servings.

Sweet Pasta Fritters

Sfrappole

Eat Sfrappole in Bologna and Cenci in Florence. Each region has a different name for this dessert.

2 cups all-purpose flour
2 eggs
1/4 cup butter, very soft for
   hand mixing, cold and in
   small pieces for food processor

1/3 cup granulated sugar
3 tablespoons rum
3 to 4 tablespoons chilled sweet white wine
Oil for frying
Powdered sugar or honey

Place flour on a wooden board and make a well in the center. Break eggs into well and beat lightly with a fork. Add butter, granulated sugar, rum and wine. Mix thoroughly with eggs. Using your hands, gradually add flour starting from inside of well and work into a ball. If using a food processor, place flour, eggs, butter, sugar and rum in processor. Using a metal blade, process until ingredients are blended. Add wine and process until dough forms a ball. Wrap dough in waxed paper and refrigerate 20 to 25 minutes. Roll out dough 1/8 inch thick. Using a pastry wheel or a sharp knife, cut dough into strips 3/4 inch wide and 6 or 7 inches long. Tie strips into bows. Pour oil 2 inches deep in a large saucepan or deep-fryer. Heat oil to 375F (190C) or until a 1-inch cube of bread turns golden brown almost immediately. Using a slotted spoon, lower pasta bows a few at a time into hot oil. Turn bows. When golden brown on both sides, remove from oil with slotted spoon. Drain on paper towels. Arrange drained bows on a platter and dust generously with powdered sugar, or drizzle with honey. Serve at room temperature. Makes 10 to 12 servings.

Baked Apples with Custard Cream

Mele Cotte alla Crema Pasticcera

The combination of piping hot apples and custard makes this an ideal winter dessert.

8 large Golden Delicious apples
1/4 cup butter
1/2 cup Marsala wine or sherry

1/2 cup sugar
Custard Cream, see below

Custard Cream:
2 cups milk
Few drops of vanilla extract
6 egg yolks

6 tablespoons sugar
1/4 cup all-purpose flour

Preheat oven to 350F (175C). Butter a large shallow baking dish. Core apples. Fill each apple with 1/2 tablespoon butter, 1 tablespoon Marsala or sherry and 1 tablespoon sugar. Place apples in buttered baking dish. Bake 40 to 50 minutes or until apple skins begin to split. While apples are baking prepare Custard Cream. Place baked apples on a serving dish. Spoon hot custard cream over each apple. Serve hot or at room temperature. Makes 8 servings.

Custard Cream:
Bring milk to a boil with vanilla in a medium saucepan. In a large heavy saucepan off the heat, beat egg yolks and sugar until pale and thick. Beat in flour until well blended. Very slowly pour in hot milk, beating constantly. Cook custard cream over medium heat 5 to 8 minutes, beating constantly. Do not boil. Custard cream is done when it coats the back of a spoon.

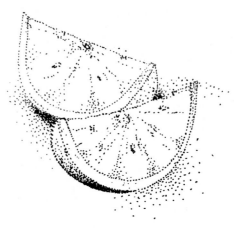

Lemon Cream

Crema al Limone

Try this cream by itself or over fresh fruit.

1 cup whipping cream
Grated zest of 1 lemon
1/4 cup sugar

Juice of 1 lemon
1/4 cup brandy

Whip cream until stiff in a medium bowl. Thoroughly fold in lemon zest, sugar, lemon juice and brandy. If cream becomes too thin after the addition of brandy, whip again. Refrigerate until ready to use. Makes 4 servings.

Baked Stuffed Peaches

Pesche Ripiene al Forno

Amaretto di Saronno cookies are found in Italian specialty stores.

6 firm ripe peaches
1/2 cup sugar
1/2 cup sliced blanched almonds
6 large Amaretto di Saronno cookies or
   almond macaroons, broken

1 egg yolk
1/3 cup Amaretto di Saronno liqueur or
   other liqueur

Preheat oven to 350F (175C). Butter a large shallow baking dish. Wash and dry peaches and cut into halves. Remove pits and scoop out not more than 1 tablespoon pulp from each half. In a blender or food processor fitted with a metal blade, combine peach pulp, sugar, almonds, almond cookies, egg yolk and liqueur. Blend to a fine paste. Divide mixture between peach halves. Arrange peaches in a single layer in buttered baking dish. Bake 20 to 25 minutes. Serve warm or at room temperature. Makes 6 servings.

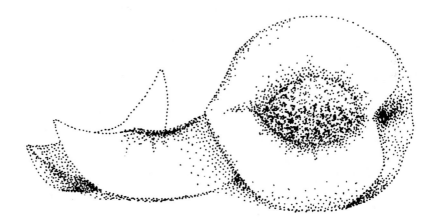

Pears Poached in Red Wine

Pere al Vino Rosso

In Italy, wine and fruit are often combined into desserts like this one.

8 firm ripe pears, preferably Bosc
4 cups good dry red wine
1 cup Marsala wine or sherry

3/4 cup sugar
Grated zest of 1 lemon
Juice of 1 lemon

Peel pears leaving stems attached. Flatten the pear bottoms by cutting off a thin slice from each. Stand pears close together in a large saucepan or casserole. Add red wine, Marsala or sherry, 1/2 cup sugar and lemon zest. Bring to a boil. Reduce heat to medium and cover pan. Cook pears 25 to 30 minutes or until tender, basting several times during cooking. Place pears in a glass bowl or platter. Let stand at room temperature until ready to serve. Add 1/4 cup sugar and lemon juice to liquid in pan. Boil until it has the consistency of syrup, 15 to 20 minutes. Spoon hot sauce over pears and serve. Makes 8 servings.

Jam Tart

Crostata di Marmellata

White wine adds a subtle flavor to this pastry.

Sweet Pie Pastry, see below
1 (12-oz.) jar strawberry jam or other jam

1 egg, lightly beaten

Sweet Pie Pastry:
2 cups all-purpose flour
2/3 cup butter, room temperature for
   hand mixing, cold and in
   small pieces for food processor

1 egg
2 tablespoons sugar
3 to 4 tablespoons chilled white wine

Prepare Sweet Pie Pastry. Butter a 10-inch tart pan with a removable bottom. Preheat oven to 375F (190C). Reserve one-third of pastry dough for lattice decoration. On a lightly floured surface, roll out remaining dough to a 12-inch circle. Carefully place dough in buttered tart pan. Trim edges of dough by gently pressing the rolling pin over top of pan. Prick bottom of pastry shell several times with a fork. Spread jam in pastry shell. Roll out reserved dough 1/8 inch thick. Using a pastry cutter or sharp knife, cut dough into 3/4-inch strips. Lay strips across tart to make a lattice, joining strips where necessary. Brush dough with beaten egg. Bake 30 to 40 minutes or until crust is golden brown. Let stand at least 30 minutes before removing from pan. Cut into thin slices. Makes 10 servings.

Sweet Pie Pastry:
In a medium bowl using a pastry blender or in a food processor fitted with a metal blade, mix flour and butter until crumbly. Add egg, sugar and wine; mix until dough is completely moistened. Place dough on a flat surface and work into a ball. Wrap in waxed paper and refrigerate at least 1 hour.

How to Make Jam Tart

1/Cut dough into 3/4-inch strips.

2/Lay strips across tart to make a lattice.

Almond Cake

Torta di Mandorle

This cake will keep several days without refrigeration.

1 pkg. active dry yeast
1/3 cup warm water (110F, 43C)
1 cup blanched almonds
3 eggs, lightly beaten
1/2 cup butter, room temperature

Grated zest of 1 lemon
3/4 cup granulated sugar
1-1/2 cups self-rising flour
Powdered sugar

Preheat oven to 350F (175C). Butter an 8-inch cake pan with a removable bottom. Stir yeast into warm water until dissolved. Chop almonds into very small pieces. In a large bowl or food processor fitted with a metal blade, combine eggs, butter, lemon zest, granulated sugar, flour, yeast mixture and almonds. Mix thoroughly. Pour batter into buttered pan. Bake 30 to 40 minutes or until cake is golden. Cool in pan 30 minutes. Place cake on a platter and dust with powdered sugar. Serve at room temperature. Makes 10 servings.

Strawberry Mousse

Spuma di Fragole

A perfect dessert for a summer dinner party.

8 cups strawberries (about 4 baskets)
3/4 cup sugar
1/2 cup Marsala wine or 1/3 cup liquor
Juice of 1 lemon
3 envelopes unflavored gelatin

1/2 cup hot water
1-1/2 cups whipping cream
Additional strawberries
Whipped cream

Wash and hull 8 cups strawberries. In a blender or food processor fitted with a metal blade, puree strawberries and sugar. Place strawberry mixture in a large bowl and stir in Marsala or liquor, and lemon juice. Stir gelatin into hot water until dissolved. Stir into strawberry mixture. Whip 1-1/2 cups cream to medium-thick; fold into strawberry mixture. Pour mousse into a large glass bowl or spoon into individual glasses. Refrigerate overnight. Before serving, decorate with additional strawberries and whipped cream. Serve chilled. Makes 10 servings.

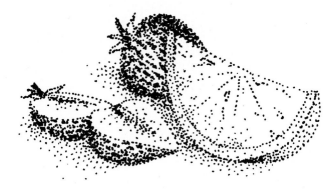

Chocolate Mousse

Spuma di Cioccolata

For an excitingly different taste, add three or four tablespoons of orange-flavored liqueur or rum.

8 oz. semisweet chocolate,
   cut into small pieces
3 eggs

1 cup whipping cream
Whipped cream
Grated chocolate

Preheat oven to 200F (95C). Put chocolate pieces into a small ovenproof bowl and place in oven until chocolate has melted, 4 to 5 minutes. Remove chocolate from oven and set aside to cool slightly. Beat eggs until foamy in a medium bowl. Beat 1 cup cream until stiff in a large bowl. Add eggs, a little at a time to cooled chocolate, beating at low speed. Do not overbeat. Fold chocolate mixture thoroughly into whipped cream. Spoon mousse into a large glass bowl or into individual glasses. Decorate with additional whipped cream and grated chocolate. Refrigerate overnight. Serve chilled. Makes 6 servings.

Almond & Pine Nut Cake

Torta di Mandorle e Pignoli

In Italy, this cake is dipped by the slice in dessert wine.

2 cups all-purpose flour
3/4 cup butter, room temperature for
  hand mixing, cold and in
  small pieces for food processor
1 egg, lightly beaten

1/2 cup sugar
1/2 cup pine nuts, finely chopped
1/2 cup blanched almonds, finely chopped
Grated zest of 1 lemon
1 to 2 tablespoons sugar

Preheat oven to 375F (190C). Butter an 8-inch cake pan with a removable bottom. In a medium bowl using a pastry blender or in a food processor fitted with a metal blade, mix flour and butter until crumbly. Add egg, 1/2 cup sugar, pine nuts, almonds and lemon zest. Using your hands or food processor, work batter into a soft ball. Spread in buttered pan with a spatula. Sprinkle 1 to 2 tablespoons sugar over batter. Bake 30 minutes or until cake is golden brown. Cool in pan 30 minutes. Place cake on a platter. Serve at room temperature. Makes 8 to 10 servings.

Family-Style Apple Cake

Torta di Mele alla Casalinga

A splendid cake for any occasion.

1 pkg. active dry yeast
1/3 cup warm water (110F, 43C)
3 eggs
1/2 cup sugar

1/2 cup butter, room temperature
2 cups self-rising flour
4 large apples, cored, peeled, thinly sliced
1 to 2 tablespoons sugar

Preheat oven to 375F (190C). Butter and flour a 10-inch cake pan with a removable bottom. Stir yeast into warm water until dissolved. Beat eggs and 1/2 cup sugar in a large bowl until pale and thick. Beat in butter, flour and yeast mixture. Add three-quarters of the apples to batter; mix with a spatula. Pour batter into buttered pan. Arrange remaining apple slices over batter. Sprinkle 1 to 2 tablespoons sugar over batter. Bake 35 to 45 minutes or until cake is golden. Cool to room temperature, then remove cake from pan. This cake keeps well in the refrigerator for several days. Return to room temperature before serving. Makes 8 to 10 servings.

Variation
Substitute 5 large pears for the apples.

Peach Tart

Crostata di Pesche

A great way to take advantage of an abundant harvest.

Sweet Pie Pastry, see below
1 egg white, lightly beaten

5 firm ripe peaches
Apricot Glaze, see below

Sweet Pie Pastry:
1-1/2 cups all-purpose flour
1/2 cup butter, room temperature for
hand mixing, cold and in
small pieces for food processor

1 egg
2 tablespoons sugar
3 to 4 tablespoons chilled white wine

Apricot Glaze:
1 cup apricot preserves
1/3 cup brandy

Prepare Sweet Pie Pastry. Butter a 10-inch tart pan with a removable bottom. Preheat oven to 400F (205C). On a lightly floured surface, roll out dough to a 12-inch circle. Place dough carefully in buttered tart pan. Trim edges of dough by gently pressing the rolling pin over top of pan. Prick bottom of pastry shell several times with a fork. Line pastry shell with aluminum foil and fill foil with uncooked rice. Bake 20 minutes. Remove foil and rice. Brush dough with egg white and bake 5 to 10 minutes longer. Fill a medium saucepan half full with water. Bring water to a boil. Add peaches and cook over high heat 60 seconds. Place in a bowl of cold water. Peel and halve peaches. Dry thoroughly. Remove pits and cut fruit into slices. Prepare Apricot Glaze. Brush pastry shell with hot Apricot Glaze. Arrange sliced peaches in shell and brush peaches with glaze. Cool in pan, then remove from pan. Refrigerate at least 2 hours before serving. Serve at room temperature. Makes 8 to 10 servings.

Sweet Pie Pastry:
In a medium bowl using a pastry blender or in a food processor fitted with a metal blade, mix flour and butter until crumbly. Add egg, sugar and wine; mix until dough is completely moistened. Place dough on a flat surface and work into a ball. Wrap in waxed paper and refrigerate at least 1 hour.

Apricot Glaze:
Combine apricot preserves and brandy in a small saucepan. Bring to a boil over medium heat. Cook about 5 minutes. Press mixture through a sieve. Glaze should not stand too long or it will become too firm. To bring it back to coating consistency, return it to heat and stir until soft.

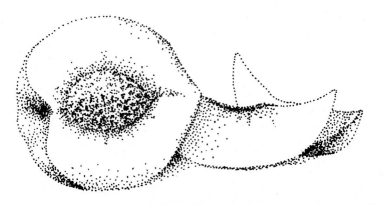

Rice Cake

Torta di Riso

Rice cake is a specialty of Bologna, and from Bologna with love, I want to share this cake with you.

4-1/2 cups milk
1-1/2 cups sugar
Grated zest of 1 lemon
3/4 cup arborio rice, page 6, or
   other short-grain rice
5 eggs

1/2 cup blanched almonds, finely chopped
1/2 cup candied citron, finely chopped
1/4 cup rum
2 to 3 tablespoons rum
Whipped cream

Preheat oven to 350F (175C). Butter a 10-inch cake pan with a removable bottom. Sprinkle pan with fine unflavored breadcrumbs and shake off excess crumbs. Combine milk, sugar and lemon zest in a medium saucepan; bring to a boil. Stir in rice and reduce heat. Simmer uncovered 45 minutes to 1 hour or until all the liquid is absorbed. Remove from heat and let cool. Beat eggs until foamy in a large bowl. Add cooled rice mixture, almonds, candied citron and 1/4 cup rum. Mix thoroughly. Pour rice mixture into buttered pan and level top with a spatula. Bake 40 to 45 minutes or until a wooden pick inserted in center of cake comes out dry. Pierce holes in top of cake with a fork and sprinkle with 2 to 3 tablespoons rum. Cool to room temperature, then remove cake from pan. Decorate with whipped cream. Makes 6 to 8 servings.

Sweet Spinach & Cheese Cake

Erbazzone Dolce all'Emiliana

Omit sugar and liqueur and you will have a perfect luncheon dish.

Sweet Pie Pastry, page 168
1-1/2 (10-oz.) pkgs. frozen spinach
1-1/2 cups blanched almonds
1 cup granulated sugar
1 lb. ricotta cheese

4 eggs, separated, room temperature
1/3 cup almond liqueur or other liqueur
Pinch of salt
1 tablespoon granulated sugar
Powdered sugar

Prepare Sweet Pie Pastry. Preheat oven to 375F (190C). Butter a 10-inch cake pan with a removable bottom. Cook spinach according to package instructions. Squeeze spinach to remove as much moisture as possible. Finely chop spinach with a knife or in a food processor fitted with a metal blade; do not puree. Finely chop almonds. In a large bowl, combine almonds, spinach, 1 cup granulated sugar, ricotta cheese, egg yolks and liqueur; mix well. Beat egg whites, salt and 1 tablespoon granulated sugar in a medium bowl until stiff. Fold beaten whites into spinach mixture. On a lightly floured surface, roll out dough to a 13-inch circle. Place dough carefully in buttered cake pan. Pour spinach mixture into pastry shell and level the filling with a spatula. Bake 1 hour or until top of cake is golden. Cool cake in pan. Place cool cake on a platter. Sprinkle top with powdered sugar. Serve at room temperature. Makes 10 servings.

Little Corner Restaurant Cake

Dolce del Cantoncino

A rich, luscious dessert from the famous Il Cantoncino restaurant in Bologna.

Sponge Cake, see below
Custard Cream, see below
Coffee Zabaglione, page 183
1 cup sweet butter, room temperature
1 cup whipping cream

2 oz. semisweet chocolate, coarsely chopped
1/4 cup rum
1 to 1-1/2 cups chopped walnuts
9 blanched almonds

Sponge Cake:
1/4 cup butter
6 eggs, room temperature
1/2 cup sugar

1/2 teaspoon vanilla extract
1 cup all-purpose flour

Custard Cream:
3 cups milk
8 egg yolks, room temperature
1 cup sugar

1/2 teaspoon vanilla extract
3/4 cup all-purpose flour

Prepare Sponge Cake. Prepare Custard Cream. Prepare Coffee Zabaglione. Cream butter in a large bowl until pale and fluffy. Gradually add cooled zabaglione to butter, beating vigorously after each addition. Refrigerate mixture 2 to 3 minutes to stiffen slightly. Whip cream and refrigerate. Preheat oven to 200F (95C). Put chocolate into a small ovenproof bowl and place in oven until chocolate has melted, 4 to 5 minutes. Cut cake into 2 layers. Sprinkle rum over 2 cut surfaces of cake. Spread 1 layer with Custard Cream. Top with second layer. Spread zabaglione mixture evenly over top of cake. Hold cake in 1 hand and spread zabaglione mixture around sides of cake. Gently press walnuts onto sides of cake. Put whipped cream into a pastry bag fitted with a medium star tube. Pipe a cream border around edge of cake. Decorate center of cake with 9 cream rosettes. Dip almonds into melted chocolate and place on top of rosettes. Refrigerate cake until serving. Cake can be prepared up to 24 hours ahead. Let cake stand 30 minutes at room temperature before serving. Makes 8 to 10 servings.

Sponge Cake:
Preheat oven to 350F (175C). Butter and flour a 10-inch cake pan with a removable bottom; shake off excess flour. Melt butter in a small saucepan; cool slightly. Put eggs, sugar and vanilla in a large bowl. Set bowl in a larger one containing hot water or use a double boiler off the heat. Beat at high speed 10 to 12 minutes or until mixture is pale and thick and has tripled in volume. Sift flour over batter in several batches, gently folding in with a spatula after each addition. Gradually add cooled butter, folding gently until well blended. Pour batter into prepared pan. Bake 20 to 25 minutes or until a wooden pick inserted in center of cake comes out dry. Cool cake in pan 20 to 30 minutes, then transfer to a rack. Cake can be prepared 1 or 2 days ahead, covered with plastic wrap and stored at room temperature.

Custard Cream:
In a medium saucepan, bring milk just to a boil. Put egg yolks, sugar and vanilla into a medium bowl. Beat 2 to 3 minutes until mixture is pale and thick. Gradually beat in flour. Very slowly stir half the hot milk into yolk mixture. Pour mixture into pan containing remaining hot milk. Whisk over medium heat 2 to 3 minutes or until custard has a medium-thick consistency. Do not let mixture boil. Place custard in a bowl. Cover and refrigerate.

Fried Fruit

Fritto Misto di Frutta

Fresh fruit as you have never tasted it.

2 eggs, separated, room temperature	**1 teaspoon sugar**
2 tablespoons sugar	**20 to 25 strawberries**
1 tablespoon olive oil	**2 apples**
2 tablespoons brandy or rum	**2 pears**
1 cup beer	**4 bananas**
1-1/2 cups all-purpose flour	**Oil for frying**
Pinch of salt	**Sugar**

Beat egg yolks, 2 tablespoons sugar, olive oil and brandy or rum in a large bowl. Add beer and beat until blended. Gradually sift in flour, beating until batter is smooth and has the consistency of thick sour cream. Cover bowl and let batter stand at room temperature 2 to 3 hours. Beat egg whites, salt and 1 teaspoon sugar in a medium bowl until stiff. Fold beaten whites into batter. Wash and hull strawberries; dry with paper towels. Core and peel apples and pears. Peel bananas. Cut apples, pears and bananas into 1/2-inch pieces. Pour oil 2 inches deep in a large saucepan or deep-fryer. Heat oil to 375F (190C) or until a 1-inch cube of bread turns golden brown almost immediately. Dip pieces of fruit into batter. Using a slotted spoon, lower fruit a few pieces at a time into hot oil. When fruit is golden all over, remove from oil with slotted spoon. Drain on paper towels. Arrange drained fruit on a platter and sprinkle with sugar. Serve hot. Makes 6 to 8 servings.

Walnut & Honey Pie

La Bonissima

A pie from Modena, named after a medieval noblewoman who sold all her jewelry to help the poor.

Sweet Pie Pastry, page 168	**1/3 cup rum**
2-1/2 cups chopped walnuts	**1 egg, lightly beaten**
3/4 cup honey	

Prepare Sweet Pie Pastry. Divide dough into 2 balls. Wrap each in waxed paper and refrigerate at least 1 hour. On a lightly floured surface, roll out 1 ball of dough to a 12-inch circle. Carefully place dough in a 10-inch tart pan with a removable bottom. Prick bottom of pastry shell with a fork. Refrigerate pastry shell until ready to use. Preheat oven to 375F (190C). Place walnuts in a medium bowl. Add honey and rum; mix to blend. Spread walnut mixture evenly in pastry shell. Roll out remaining ball of dough to a 10-inch circle. Place carefully over walnut filling. Pinch edges of top dough with bottom dough to seal. Brush surface with beaten egg. Prick top of pie in 5 or 6 places with a fork. Bake 40 minutes or until crust is golden. Let stand at least 15 minutes before removing from pan and serving. Makes 8 to 10 servings.

Sweet Tortelli Emilia-Romagna-Style

Tortelli Dolci all'Emiliana

Yummy is the word to describe these sweet tortelli. Another family-style dessert and another winner.

2-1/2 cups all-purpose flour
3 eggs
1/3 cup granulated sugar
Grated zest of 1 lemon
1/2 cup butter, very soft for
   hand mixing, cold and in
   small pieces for food processor

1/3 cup chilled white wine
Strawberry jam or other jam
Oil for frying
Powdered sugar

Place flour on a pastry board and make a well in the center. Break eggs into well and beat lightly with a fork. Add granulated sugar, lemon zest, butter and wine. Mix thoroughly with eggs. Using your hands, gradually add flour starting from inside of well and work into a ball. If using a food processor, place flour, eggs, sugar, lemon zest and butter in processor. Using a metal blade, process until ingredients are blended. Add wine and process until dough forms a ball. Wrap dough in waxed paper and refrigerate 1 hour. On a lightly floured surface, roll out dough 1/8 inch thick. Using a 3-inch round scalloped pastry cutter or a glass, cut dough into circles. Put 1 heaping teaspoon jam into each circle of dough. Fold each circle in half and press edges firmly. Pour oil 2 inches deep in a large saucepan or deep-fryer. Heat oil to 375F (190C) or until a 1-inch cube of bread turns golden brown almost immediately. Using a slotted spoon, lower tortelli a few at a time into hot oil. Turn tortelli. When golden brown on both sides, remove from oil with slotted spoon. Drain on paper towels. Arrange drained tortelli on a platter and sprinkle with powdered sugar. Serve hot. Makes 8 to 10 servings.

Hot Zabaglione

Zabaglione Caldo

A classic Italian dessert that needs no introduction.

8 egg yolks
1/2 cup sugar

3/4 cup dry Marsala wine, sherry or port

In a large bowl or the top part of a double boiler, beat egg yolks and sugar until pale and thick. Set bowl or top part of double boiler over simmering water; do not let water boil. Add Marsala, sherry or port slowly, beating constantly. Zabaglione is ready when mixture has tripled in volume and it is soft and fluffy, after 4 to 6 minutes. Spoon into individual glasses. Serve immediately. Makes 6 to 8 servings.

Variation

Cold Zabaglione (Zabaglione Freddo): As soon as Zabaglione swells up into a soft mass, set bowl or top part of a double boiler over a bowl of ice water. Continue stirring until cool. Spoon into glasses and refrigerate until ready to serve.

Sweet Fried Cream Photo on pages 180 and 181.

Crema Fritta

Transform staple ingredients into this delicate and delicious dessert.

2 cups milk	**1-1/2 cups very fine, dry**
6 egg yolks	**unflavored breadcrumbs**
6 tablespoons granulated sugar	**2 eggs, lightly beaten**
Grated zest of 1 lemon	**Oil for frying**
1/4 cup all-purpose flour	**1/3 cup powdered sugar**

Bring milk to a boil in a medium saucepan. In a large heavy saucepan off the heat, beat egg yolks, granulated sugar and lemon zest until pale and thick. Beat in flour until well blended. Very slowly pour in hot milk, beating constantly. Cook custard cream over medium heat 5 to 8 minutes, beating constantly. Do not let boil. Custard cream is done when it coats the back of a spoon. Moisten a large plate or cookie sheet with water. Spread cooked cream to a thickness of 1/2 to 1 inch. Cream can be prepared to this point a day or two ahead. When cream is completely cooled, cut into squares or diamonds. Place breadcrumbs in a shallow dish. Coat cream shapes with breadcrumbs. Dip coated cream shapes into beaten eggs, and coat again with breadcrumbs. Pour oil 2 inches deep in a large saucepan or deep-fryer. Heat oil to 375F (190C) or until a 1-inch cube of bread turns golden brown almost immediately. Using a slotted spoon, lower cream pieces a few at a time into hot oil. Turn cream pieces. When golden on both sides, remove from oil with slotted spoon. Drain on paper towels. Arrange drained fried cream on a platter and sprinkle with powdered sugar. Serve hot. Makes 6 to 8 servings.

Oranges in Liqueur Photo on pages 180 and 181.

Arance al Liquore

Oranges combined with liqueur make a perfect light ending to a robust meal.

Zest of 1 orange, thinly sliced	**1/3 cup sugar**
6 large oranges	**1/4 cup Cointreau or brandy**
1/2 cup chopped walnuts	**Juice of 1 orange**
2 tablespoons butter	

Fill a small saucepan one-third full with water. Bring water to a boil. Add orange zest and boil 3 to 5 minutes to reduce bitterness. Drain and dry well with paper towels. Cut ends off oranges. Set each orange on a cutting board and slice off peel, making sure to remove all white skin. Cut oranges into slices about 1/3 inch thick. Remove seeds. Arrange orange slices slightly overlapping on a large platter or in individual dishes. Sprinkle oranges with walnuts and set aside. Melt butter in a small saucepan. Stir in sugar, orange zest and Cointreau or brandy. Stir over medium heat until sugar is dissolved. Add orange juice. Cook, stirring occasionally, until sauce is a medium-thick consistency. Spoon over oranges and serve. Makes 4 to 6 servings.

Variation

Arrange sliced oranges on a platter or individual dishes and sprinkle with walnuts. Squeeze the juice of 1 large lemon over oranges and sprinkle with 1/3 cup sugar. Chill 20 to 30 minutes and serve.

How to Make Sweet Fried Cream

1/Coat cream squares with breadcrumbs.

2/Using a slotted spoon, lower squares into hot oil.

Raspberry Sauce with Liqueur

Salsa di Lamponi al Liquore

Serve this sauce over vanilla ice cream or pound cake.

2 cups fresh or thawed frozen raspberries   **1/3 cup any fruit liqueur**
1/2 cup sugar

Drain frozen raspberries if using. In a blender or food processor fitted with a metal blade, combine raspberries, sugar and liqueur and blend to a thick sauce. To remove seeds, press sauce through a sieve and into a glass bowl. Refrigerate until ready to use. Makes 8 servings.

A menu typical of the Emilia-Romagna region is shown on pages 180 and 181. Clockwise starting from center top, Green Tagliatelle with Tomato Sauce, page 36; Prosciutto with Melon, page 13; Stuffed Artichokes, page 138; Baked Tomatoes, page 133; Stuffed Veal Roast, page 118; Buttered Carrots, page 141; Oranges in Liqueur, page 178; and Sweet Fried Cream, page 178.

Italian Rum Cake

Zuppa Inglese

This is one of Italy's most popular desserts.

Fruit Salad, see below
Zabaglione, see below
12 oz. pound cake, cut into
   medium-thin slices

1/2 cup rum
Fresh strawberries, grated chocolate

Fruit Salad:
5 cups any prepared fruit in season
1/2 cup chopped candied fruit

2 tablespoons rum
3 tablespoons sugar

Zabaglione:
8 egg yolks
1/2 cup sugar

1/3 cup rum
1 cup whipping cream

Prepare Fruit Salad and Zabaglione. Arrange slices of pound cake in a large glass bowl. Sprinkle a little rum over each slice. Cover cake with a layer of Fruit Salad. Cover Fruit Salad with a generous amount of Zabaglione. Continue layers until bowl is filled. Refrigerate overnight. Before serving, decorate with fresh strawberries and/or grated chocolate. Serve chilled. Makes 10 to 12 servings.

Fruit Salad:

Combine fresh fruit, candied fruit, rum and sugar in a medium bowl. Refrigerate until ready to use. Fruit Salad can be prepared several hours ahead.

Zabaglione:

In a large bowl or the top part of a double boiler, beat egg yolks and sugar until pale and thick. Set bowl or top part of double boiler over simmering water. Do not let water boil. Gradually add rum, beating constantly. Continue beating until Zabaglione has doubled in volume and is soft and fluffy, 4 to 6 minutes. Remove from heat and set pan or bowl containing mixture over a bowl full of ice water. Stir with a whisk until mixture is warm. Whip cream and fold it into warm mixture. Zabaglione can be prepared several hours ahead and set over a bowl of ice water until needed.

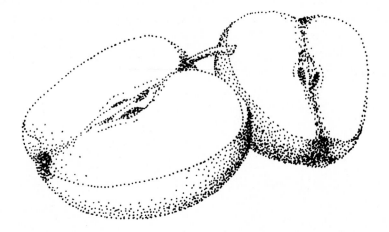

Maria Angela's Meringue Cake

Dolce di Maria Angela

This is a family favorite from my good friend Maria Angela di Massa.

Italian Meringues, see below
Coffee Zabaglione, see below

1 cup sweet butter, room temperature
Candied violets

Italian Meringues:
4 egg whites, room temperature
1 cup sugar

1 teaspoon vanilla extract
1 teaspoon white wine vinegar

Coffee Zabaglione:
5 egg yolks
1 cup sugar

1/4 cup espresso coffee or strong
regular coffee, room temperature

Prepare Italian Meringues. Prepare Coffee Zabaglione. Cream butter in a large bowl until pale and fluffy. Gradually add cooled zabaglione to butter, beating vigorously after each addition. Refrigerate 2 to 3 minutes to stiffen slightly. On a large round platter, arrange about 8 meringues close together in a circle. Put zabaglione mixture into a pastry bag fitted with a medium star tube. Pipe rosettes between meringues. Arrange another layer of meringues over the first, forming a smaller circle. Pipe rosettes of zabaglione mixture between meringues. Repeat layers using remaining meringues and most of zabaglione mixture to make a cone-shape mound. Decorate cake with candied violets and remaining zabaglione mixture. Refrigerate overnight. Let cake stand 30 minutes at room temperature before serving. Makes 6 to 8 servings.

Italian Meringues:
Preheat oven to 275F (135C). Butter and flour 2 cookie sheets. In a large bowl, beat egg whites until stiff. Beat in 6 tablespoons sugar, 1 tablespoon at a time. Beat in vanilla and vinegar. Add remaining sugar, beating until egg whites are very stiff and shiny. Put egg white mixture into a pastry bag fitted with a medium star tube. Pipe mixture in small mounds onto prepared cookie sheets or shape into mounds using 2 spoons. Bake 1 hour. Turn off oven. Leave meringues in oven overnight with door closed. Store meringues in an airtight container. Meringues can be stored several weeks. Makes about 25 meringues.

Coffee Zabaglione:
In a large bowl or the top part of a double boiler, beat egg yolks and sugar until pale and thick. Set bowl or top part of double boiler over simmering water; do not let water boil. Gradually add coffee, beating constantly. Continue beating until zabaglione has doubled in volume and is soft and fluffy, 4 to 6 minutes. Remove from heat and set pan or bowl over a bowl full of ice water. Stir with a whisk until mixture is cool.

*O*ne problem that confronts someone serving ethnic food for the first time is how to compose the menu. So many of my students ask me the same question: "I am planning a dinner party and I would like to make tortellini with cream sauce. What appetizer should I have and what dessert should I serve?"

The success of a meal depends not only on how well the food is prepared but also on how the menu is put together. In a way it is like listening to a beautiful piece of music. Each note can be played perfectly but the overall beauty of the sound depends on the way the notes are put together. To prepare a beautiful meal you must start by planning a beautiful menu: A menu in which each dish complements the other. One that takes advantage of seasonal ingredients and suits the mood of the time of year.

An Italian meal moves through its many courses in a leisurely and orderly sequence. Wine is always present. The right wine not only complements the meal, but enhances appreciation of it. On a hot summer day we eat differently than in winter. It would be ridiculous to spend time over a hot stove, stirring a bubbling *polenta* when the temperature outside reaches the sizzling point. On the other hand, cook a polenta on a cold winter day and you bring a warm glow to your family or guests. With this concept in mind, I have put together 11 menus for this chapter. They are divided into spring and summer, and fall and winter. These menus are intended only as guidelines because there are countless possible menu combinations using the recipes in this book.

By changing a pasta dish, by substituting meat for fish, by eliminating a course, you can create your own menus. Each combination can fit a particular occasion or season. For example, a pot of bean soup followed by broiled chicken or Chicken Hunter-Style, page 91, can become a simple yet excellent meal. Serve it for an informal gathering of friends. Why not cook several *frittatas,* make a

tomato and basil salad and fill a cheese board with assorted Italian cheeses. Then eat this delightful meal informally outdoors on your patio, by a river or at a beach. Select a stuffed pasta dish and, working around it, build an elegant meal—a meal that will linger in the minds of your guests. And let's not forget the everyday meals for our families. The same care should be taken in preparing the simplest of meals. After all, good food should not be kept in the closet and served only on special occasions. Good food belongs on the everyday table. We must all eat, so why not make the best of it?

Most Italian meals end with an unbeatable combination—cheese and fruit. Creamy Gorgonzola cheese and sweet, ripe pears is a marriage made in heaven. Fresh fruit, when ripe and sweet, can stand on its own as dessert. Of course there are many occasions when a beautiful dessert should end a meal. In formal entertaining, a spectacular dessert is not only advised, but recommended. If you plan a menu with a beautiful first course and end with an impressive dessert, you can be sure your dinner party will be a success.

To end an Italian meal without espresso coffee would be an absurdity. In Italy, espresso is a national institution. I remember when my husband first arrived in Bologna to attend medical school, he barely managed one or two cups of this strong coffee a day. By the time he graduated, he was drinking eight to ten cups a day. Today, after 20 years in this country I still start my day with several cups of espresso and end it in the same way. Many of my friends believe espresso is the source of my considerable energy.

I have included one really lavish holiday menu from Emilia-Romagna in this selection. The photo on pages 180 and 181 will show you how sensational a well-planned menu will look on your table.

It just occurred to me that this is the last chapter of this book. After working on it for more than a year, I know I will miss the daily routine of preparing recipes in my kitchen and then sitting down to write them up. I hope I have achieved what I had in mind. I set out to share with you not only some of the food of northern Italy, but also to give you a little understanding of a very old, warm and beautiful country.

Holiday Menu from Emilia-Romagna

Prosciutto with Melon, page 13
Green Tagliatelle with
Tomato Sauce, page 36
Stuffed Veal Roast, page 118
Stuffed Artichokes, page 138
Baked Tomatoes, page 133
Buttered Carrots, page 141
Oranges in Liqueur, page 178
Sweet Fried Cream, page 178
Mature Barbaresco or
*Cabernet Sauvignon

*California wine

Potato Dumplings with
Mushroom Sauce, page 60
Pan-Roasted Chicken, page 85
Peas with Prosciutto, page 136
Fresh Fruit
Jam Tart, page 168
Valpolicella or *Gamay Beaujolais

Hot Anchovy Dip, page 14
Basic Polenta, page 62, with
Rabbit with Wine & Vegetables, page 86
Mixed Salad, page 149
Pears Poached in Red Wine, page 167
Barbera or *Cabernet Sauvignon

Macaroni Pie, page 38
Pork Loin with Garlic & Rosemary, page 104
Sweet & Sour Little Onions, page 136
Fresh Fruit
Sweet Fried Cream, page 178
Merlot or *Light Zinfandel

Tortellini in Broth, page 24
Veal Cutlets Bologna-Style, page 119
Baked Tomatoes, page 133
Gorgonzola Cheese with Fresh Pears
Italian Rum Cake, page 182
Barbaresco or *Napa Zinfandel

Roasted Peppers, page 16
Risotto with Champagne, page 66
Beef Braised in Barolo Wine, page 124
Baked Fennel with Butter & Cheese, page 135
Oranges in Liqueur, page 178
Barolo or *Cabernet Sauvignon

*California wine

Trenette with Pesto Sauce, page 55
Cold Veal in Tuna Fish Sauce, page 116
Mixed Salad, page 149
Cold Zabaglione, page 177, with Fresh Strawberries
Trebbiano or *Fumé Blanc

Rice & Pea Soup, page 22
Calf's Liver in Onion Sauce, page 109
Asparagus Salad, page 148
Lemon Cream, page 166, with Fresh Fruit
Merlot, *Light Mendocino or *Zinfandel

Strichetti with Garlic & Tomato Sauce, page 42
Veal Chops Milan-Style, page 111
Mushrooms with Marsala Wine & Cream, page 132
Mixed Salad, page 149
Peach Tart, page 172
Gattinara or *Pinot Noir

Risotto with Asparagus Tips, page 71
Trout with Green Mayonnaise, page 83
Tomato Salad, page 146
Fried Fruit, page 176
Gavi dei Gavi or *Chardonnay

Prosciutto with Figs, page 13
Spaghetti with Spring Vegetables, page 48
Roast Rack of Lamb, page 99
Zucchini with Vinegar, page 130
Strawberry Mousse, page 170
Tignanello or *Cabernet Sauvignon

*California wine

Italian Recipe Titles

Italian Recipe Titles continued

Index

Index continued

Index continued